CONTENTS

Introduction

The purpose of this book is to help us deal more effectively and fruitfully with suffering in our own lives and in the lives of others. Like any educational tool, it challenges some common assumptions and clarifies others.

The first thing this book presupposes is that suffering surrounds us. The small boy slowly dying of an undetermined disease suffers. The divorced mother trying to bring up a family on her own suffers. The top-security research assistant, who cannot discuss his research with his wife, suffers. The middle-aged couple rushing from novelty to novelty suffers. Suffering is a part of life. In Part One of this book, "Singers, Songs, and Us," many singers and many songs of suffering are presented to help us become more sensitive to the suffering of others and realize how we share in their suffering.

This book is about suffering as a part of life, not isolated from it. The small boy we have mentioned laughs in the midst of his suffering. The divorced mother warms to the touch of her daughter. The research assistant goes for a Florida vacation. The middle-aged couple captures a moment of mutual love. Human suffering is part of one's entire life: past, present, and future.

Human suffering is diminished when it is recognized and shared. When the boy knows that his parents love him, the suffering diminishes. The divorcée's awareness that someone will help her lessens her suffering. The sensitivity of the researcher's wife and children to his plight fills the forced silence of their daily communication. Our awareness of other people's suffering begins the process of lessening it.

Awareness of suffering is not an occasional intellectual game but a constant reality. What you or I recognize as suffering depends upon our past and present experience of what we call suffering. Some people recognize certain situations as filled with suffering; others do not. To the majority of those reading this book, for instance, the dominant context of life probably is a considerable degree of comfort. So for them, physical suffering is an intrusion. But for the majority of people on this planet, physical suffering was and is an accepted fact of daily life.

It is because of such different contexts of suffering that each chapter in Part One begins by presenting individuals who sing the song of suffering. Many times when we talk about serious matters, we forget the origin of our discussion. Just as a bird-lover first points to a bird and then begins to tell us something about it, so it is necessary for us to point again and again to the actual situation so that we do not forget what we are discussing. This guarantees that our reflection and understanding are rooted in experience. Any talk of lessening suffering, though, must take place in union with those who suffer. If we lose contact with those who actually suffer, we may mistakenly add to their suffering while we are trying to lessen it.

A sensitive person, knowing of another's suffering, asks, "What can I do about it?" The answer seems obvious. The severe headache finds us reaching for the aspirin; we answer the question by seeking to relieve the suffering. Few of us do otherwise. The answer to the question of what to do about suffering, in this instance, is to get rid of it as quickly as possible. But just as the aspirin may relieve the headache and leave its cause untouched, so too an overly quick attempt to do something about some form of suffering before understanding the song of suffering and its cause may produce more suffering in the future. In an attempt to lessen suffering, we may unwittingly intensify it. Thus Part One treats not only the singers of suffering and their songs; it also analyzes the language of suffering and its physical, emotional, and societal causes. When we wish *to do* something about suffering, it helps *to know* something about it.

What can we do about suffering? A great deal. And so each chapter suggests ways to reduce suffering in the light of our understanding of it.

Many of us cannot experience or deal with suffering for any length of time without questioning the fortuity and the meaning of life: "Why me, and not him or her? What's the use of putting up with this pain?" Such questions examine the purpose, the comprehensibility, and the meaning of who we are and why we are. These questions suggest that the physical, emotional, and social dimensions of suffering are pieces of a larger puzzle: the ultimate meaning and significance of life itself. To speak of ultimacy, meaning, and significance is to speak of religion in general, for all religions deal with the ultimate meaning and significance of life.

Religions have always taken for granted that we do suffer; they have sought to understand it, to deal with it, to lessen it. To understand a person's religion is to understand something of that person's suffering. But none of us copes with suffering through religion "in general." No, each of us deals with suffering from one particular religious perspective. Consequently, in Part Two I discuss how Christian experience understands and copes with suffering. You may share some of this Christian perspective and concern and yet feel that some of what I say is new to you. It should be new, because what you read is the result of much discussion, thought, and shared suffering. Many people have taught me their song of suffering and waited patiently for me to understand it.

One person in particular has been my teacher in the last year of writing this book: my son who had an inoperable brain tumor. His smile taught me how to transcend limitation; his confidence, how to trust; his gradually increasing deformity, how to see true beauty; his joy in simple knowledge, how liberating learning can be.

He unintentionally suggested the title of this book. As a small child, he amused my wife and me by his "singing." This singing was a mixture of notes, more or less, and words, less rather than more. But notes and words poured from his lips and heart seeking a parent's reward. A clap, a nod, a laugh from us was enough. Then, when he was five years old, he was diagnosed as having an inoperable brain tumor. Sickness and drugs destroyed the spontaneity of his song but did not stop his singing. When we were singing together, we could hear him joining us. For a moment, song conquered suffering. As I reflected on these youthful human experiences, the relationship of life, suffering, and song became clear.

Each of us has a song to sing. To speak of someone's song is to speak of his or her style of life. We sing a suffering song when suffering is the dominant melody of our life. This melody determines how others experience us as well as how we know ourselves. I invite you to listen to the songs contained here. They offer an insight about life we seldom have an opportunity to reflect upon.

I thank my wife Judy, who has always been willing to share her song with me and allow me to sing mine; and David and Sharon, whose songs, when raucous, provided necessary distractions; when harmonious, provided an atmosphere for thought. I thank too Nathan "Rudy" Kollar, Jr., for his suggestions as well as his life: He sang a beautiful song.

* * *

Each chapter of this book will end with questions designed to stimulate individual and group reflection. The purpose of these questions is to deepen your awareness of the songs of suffering. To get the most out of what is being discussed in this book, both individual and group reflection are necessary.

The suggestions for individual reflection can best be carried out as follows: Buy a notebook or a diary. Read each question and jot down ideas as they come to you before you begin to filter them through your fears, images, expectations. No need for complete sentences; just jot down your ideas when they come. Then go back over them and reflect on what you have written. Perhaps you can share these intimate reflections with someone you trust.

Any group concerned with physical, emotional, or social suffering can use this book with great benefit. For instance, groups made up of cancer patients and their families will be challenged to look at themselves as part of a larger community of suffering. On the other hand, those groups dealing with the global causes of suffering, such as nuclear war, will discover in this book not only ways of attacking those world problems but ways of looking at the face of individual sufferers.

The groups can meet in homes, hospitals, churches, or organizational headquarters. Meetings must be held regularly, about once a week. The group reflections are designed to give everyone an opportunity to express his or her mind and feelings in regard to the matter at hand. But no one should be forced to say what he or she feels. Freedom should be the keynote of each discussion group: freedom to speak, to listen, to act, or to be silent. My hope is that through these chapters, and the reflections upon them, we can discover the moments of song and diminish the threat of being without any song to sing.

PART ONE

Singers, Songs, and Us

Introduction to Part One

Each of us is a singer. A blink of an eye, a tap of a toe, a handshake, a shout of despair can be the notes that make up our song. We sing from the first cry of life to its last breath. Between the cry of birth and the silence of death are laughs and arguments, curses, exclamations of joy, quiet whispers of love, loud protestations against injustice. With each of these we search for an appreciative audience to respond to our song as we sing it.

Song is used here as a symbol of our life. Our song is the way we live and the way we express ourselves to others. It is true, of course, that there is something unique and incommunicable about each of us. Yet through our song we try to communicate to others our feelings, thoughts, and values. All the people around us have their own songs to sing to us. In Part One we listen to the singers of suffering, try to understand their songs, and suggest ways to change their songs of suffering to songs of joy.

The singer or sufferer, as we have mentioned, is unique. No one can completely understand the suffering of another. Deep within us we know that suffering is a mystery, but sometimes we forget. Especially those of us who are professionals may easily forget. We are trained to look for causes. If we deal with the physical, psychological, or social dimensions of suffering, we look for *the* cause of the suffering. One suffers "because of" this disease, "because of" this emotional upset, "because of" this social structure. This identification of suffering with one of its causes is a constant temptation in a society that is reductionistic by nature. Suffering is much more complex than the purveyors of reductionistic solutions would lead us to believe. A *person* suffers. Each of us is more than our body, more than our emotions, more than our relationships to others. We are more than the "parts" or "causes" that many serious professionals tend to reduce us to. We are more than the sum of our parts. In fact, we are not parts at all. We are persons, not machines. Using language that suggests we are things rather than persons sometimes leads us to forget our holistic nature, and we tend to identify ourselves with a body part such as our brain or our heart. We may forget that *we* sing—not just our voice, our lips, or our mouth. *We* are singers.

We suffer—not just our toe, our emotions, or our relationship with others. Yet it can be useful to speak of these dimensions of ourselves without for the moment paying much attention to the other dimensions. Such a focus of speech or of research can be of great help in reducing or taking away a particular cause of suffering. In Part One we will focus in turn upon the physical, emotional, and communal dimensions of the sufferer as an expression of the way a person suffers. This will enable us to concern ourselves with particular ways of dealing with suffering while remaining conscious of our holistic nature.

An example of our holistic nature is found in our description of the relationship between pain and suffering. In the Superbowl, for instance, both teams experience pain, but when the final gun sounds only one team experiences suffering. *Suffering* is a word used to refer to what happens to the whole person; *pain* refers to certain physical reactions in a person. Thus the words, as used here, are not synonymous. As we will see, all suffering involves pain, but not all pain necessarily involves suffering. We must keep in mind, therefore, that as we speak of the songs of physical, emotional, or communal suffering, we cannot speak of one of these without speaking of the others. Furthermore, to read about the song of suffering is to be one step away from the singer of the song. To speak of one of these songs without speaking of the others is to forget the singer.

A song implies pattern, cohesiveness, melody. Once we sing our song it takes on a life of its own: Some people hear it one way; others, another way. A song of suffering is our way of suffering. A song has many meanings, many contexts, and many levels of intensity. It affects the whole person and depends upon a specific context to be understood. For instance, the song "You Are My Sunshine" is familiar to many. "Sunshine" might refer to a person or an animal. We might hear or sing this song in a romantic mood when we first fall in love; in a sad mood when our lover is sick; in an angry mood when he or she has left us. To know the way the singer is singing the song, we must know more than the words or melody.

A song of suffering is much the same as an ordinary song: Only when we know the singer do we have an awareness of what *this* song means right now. The intensity of the song of suffering also demands that we be sensitive to more than its language and patterns. What may seem to one person an insignificant aspect of a song of suffering may seem overwhelming to another. The loss of hair in some treatments for cancer may be insignificant to a man whose male family members are bald, but it is usually overwhelming to a teenage girl. Context is always important. In Part One we speak of singers, songs, the language of suffering, common misunderstandings of physical, emotional, and communal suffering, and ways to reduce suffering. Throughout that discussion we must remember that the context of the sufferer determines the intensity of the suffering. This context is formed from everything that goes to make up the singer's life. With this understanding we can see why a hand extended in love may be as important as one offering an analgesic.

Each of us can reach out to the sufferer. Each of us who suffers can willingly accept the love and concern of others. We can share the song of suffering. As limited and sinful human beings we are a community of sufferers seeking to lessen the suffering that surrounds us. Religion enables us to see beyond our own limitations. It offers redemption of our sins. Part One ends with a confirmation of finitude or limit. Part Two looks at suffering as a whole. Beyond the singer, the songs, and ourselves is a perspective of the whole that religion alone can provide. But to realize that perspective we must first hear the songs of suffering.

CHAPTER ONE

Songs of Our Body: Physical Suffering

Singers

The small child stood there, tears running down his cheeks. "I can't sing," he pleaded. The teacher, ruler in hand, declared: "Everyone can sing. Begin!" And pointing to the notes chalked on the board, she struck the child's backside every time he missed a note.

Joe was a thirty-three-year-old medical student. I first met him flat on his back in a hospital bed. As we talked he described how he felt about his condition. He always had difficulty making decisions; he said it was because he was afraid of hurting people. He feared the power of his words and actions. Now he was in a hospital threatened with a future of pain and a slow death. I had to leave town for a week. When I returned, Joe had taken a turn for the worse: Tubes were coming out of every orifice in his body; machines were monitoring his vital signs. He was conscious, but a minor surgery on his throat prevented him from speaking. Slowly he wrote "Damn!"

Marie has a twinkle in her eye. Like the first star in the night sky, it twinkles alone, attracting attention, helping us forget her prognosis. A petite girl of five, she begins school next year. We were talking with her parents, helping them understand Marie's illness. Right now it was in remission. She played, jumped, and ran like any of the other children on the block. But more and more frequently, she would be faced with extended stays in the hospital. She knows that something makes her feel weak and unable to keep her food down. But she is confident her parents will take care of her.

A small boy, head hairless and marked with scars, turns to shake hands at the kiss of peace. No hand clasps his. Each person, ignoring the reality in his or her midst, turns to a healthy brother or sister in Christ and shakes hands. The child, hand outstretched, turns to one, to another, and another. . . . Too busy with sharing Christ's peace, they ignore Christ's suffering. The young child pulls at the pantleg of a young man. The young man looks, forces a smile, awkwardly and quickly shakes hands.

Now others notice the boy. They shake his hand and look away. The child smiles and tries to continue shaking hands. Full of joy, he moves from one to another. "I'm grown up. Look, they're shaking my hand," he says loudly to his father.

* * *

Physical suffering has many singers. Who is the significant singer of these songs in your life? Who first comes to mind when you think of physical suffering? That person and the many others suggested by these examples are singers of the songs of physical suffering.

Songs

There are many songs of physical suffering. Five of these may be described as: "It only hurts a little while"; "I'm feeling better, but I'll never be the same"; "It hurts and hurts"; "Something's wrong, but we don't know what"; "I'm going to die."

1. *"It only hurts a little while."* This song flows from the pain we feel when, for example, the dentist drills a tooth, a winter cold puts us to bed, or we strain a muscle or break a bone. These are instances when we know that with time and care this particular pain or illness will pass away. This kind of ailment is a training in patience more than anything else. Yet in a society where time is money, these pains or illnesses are very exasperating, especially if they come at inopportune moments.

We must remember that what might seem a slight inconvenience to some of us may be a serious disruption of life for someone else. For a toy salesman to have a serious cold in July is one thing; to have it during the Christmas season is something else. This shortlived illness actually affects the salesman's salary for the rest of the year. This song of physical suffering is one instance of how difficult it is to understand the suffering of another person.

2. *"I'm feeling better, but I'll never be the same."* This song arises from such events as serious accidents, operations that take away one of our body parts, or radiation treatments that cause loss of hair, appetite, or sexual potency. For whatever reason—physical, social, or mental—the physical change results in a new way of liv-

ing. Maybe we will need medication for the rest of our life, or maybe we have a mechanical part where there used to be flesh and blood. The realization that we have lost part of our self and the fear that we are consequently someone different hovers on the edge of our consciousness. For example, as the result of a car wreck a young man might always have to walk with a cane, so somehow he will never again be his former physical self. When we know someone who sings this song, we sometimes forget the pain that remains after the crisis is over. When we discover that the person survived the car wreck, we are relieved. Even the joy of seeing him alive and walking with a cane sometimes makes us forget that even though he is better, he is not the same.

3. *"It hurts and hurts."* This is the song of those who experience pain for prolonged periods of time. The growing pains of adolescence or the arthritis during old age are instances of these songs. The more chronic types of pain are also part of this song. Whether it is a tension headache that appears with intensity and regularity, or difficulty in breathing when embarrassed, or back pain with no known cause, or a sinus problem when it rains, we somehow learn to cope with such pains. They become part of our life-style. Those who live with us realize than when it rains we will be tense because of sinus pain. It always hurts. What is important in dealing with this song is to realize that there are those who live for prolonged periods of time in pain. Some persons might suggest that this type of pain is "psychological," meaning that it exists only in our minds or is just part of living through a particular stage of human development (e.g., old age). But to those who hurt, it is not in the mind. It hurts and hurts.

4. *"Something's wrong, but we don't know what."* Here, the person has symptoms that no one understands fully. The medical doctors either do not know what causes these symptoms, or they know many possible causes for them. The result is that they cannot help us because they do not have enough information. This medical ignorance leaves the sufferer and the medical staff waiting for what happens next. The physical suffering must increase in order for the sumptoms to become clearer. The person suffers without even the comfort of knowing the cause of the suffering.

5. *"I'm going to die."* Any song of physical suffering might result in complications that can cause death, even though this does not ordinarily happen. But when we realize we have an illness that usually results in death we sing this song.

We must remember that this is a song of living as well as dying. In *The Experience of Dying* (Englewood Cliffs, N.J.: Prentice-Hall, 1977), E. Pattison describes life after the discovery of a terminal illness as the living-dying interval. When we realize that we will die as a consequence of our illness, and face that illness aware of the importance of life as well as death, we sing this song. The emphasis is upon life while we are conscious of death. Every day counts for singing. The danger is that we and those around us will focus too easily upon the death present in our song, not upon our life. Remember that although some are singing the song, "I'm going to die," they *are* singing!

This brief description of these songs and singers suggests some of the many ways in which physical pain is the source of suffering. Every newscast and newspaper shows us more songs. Yet no matter which song we hear, we must remain sensitive to the uniqueness of the individual sufferer and to the song he or she sings.

Aches and Pains:
The Language of Physical Pain

Even though pain is a part of suffering, we have a difficult time arriving at a comprehensive theory of its causes and composition. Although we all experience pain, we do not agree on an understanding of it. Now we see it, now we don't. Like a magician's rabbit, it escapes our understanding while it remains clearly evident to our senses.

Acute and chronic pain are two general ways of speaking about physical pain. Acute pain is severe, sharp, and usually of short duration. Chronic pain is of long duration and frequent recurrence.

Acute pain is taken more seriously in current medical practice. It is a necessary warning signal. A child's excruciating sore throat warns parents and the doctor to be alert for a possible streptococcus infection that could cause heart damage. A middle-aged man's crushing pain in the chest and left arm is a likely and helpful warning of a heart attack. But those rare persons who never feel acute pain are in continual danger from everyday things that are too hot, too cold, too sharp, too caustic because such persons can be seriously injured or become seriously ill without realizing it in time to save themselves.

Chronic pain is another world of physical suffering. It may be present without any evident cause. It affects millions and makes life all but unbearable for them. Until recently chronic pain was neglected by scientists and physicians alike.

The trend toward viewing the patient as a person rather than as a collection of organs and symptoms is partly responsible for bringing chronic pain out of the shadows.

Chronic pain costs Americans more than 40 billion dollars a year in health-care costs and lost productivity. It is estimated, for example, that arthritis affects 21 million Americans and that more than 6 million of these are in so much pain as to be partially or totally disabled. Lower-back pain is said to afflict about 7 million adults who lose 10 to 15 million work days a year because of it. There are many other causes of chronic pain, such as headaches, digestive problems, and certain neurological disorders.

Descriptions of Why We Feel Pain

The pain in my left thumb demands interpretation. The hammer in my right hand, with its head firmly planted on the thumb, offers an interpretation: I hit the thumb! Once we move away from such obvious interpretations of why we hurt, though, understanding becomes more difficult. Nevertheless, we seek interpretation not just because we are curious but also because proper interpretation can lead to diminishment of pain. There are many interpretations of what causes the pain. For instance, in some societies pain is seen as resulting from the evil eye, the spell of a witch. Means are taken to ward off this pain; perhaps an opposing spell is cast or a lucky charm is worn. In any case the sequence is clear: cause of pain; removal of cause = removal of pain; I no longer hurt.

Our society has two principal ways of interpreting why we feel pain: the *disease model* and the *behavior model*.

We are familiar with the first. The *disease model* assumes that the hurt-feeling (pain) is under the control of something other than the hurting itself (e.g., a virus). There are three distinct steps to this interpretation: (1) The symptoms are observed: it hurts; (2) the underlying pathology or disease is identified, a diagnosis is made; (3) the pathology is attacked directly in the hope that the symptoms will disappear.

The *behavior model* claims that the context of the feeling of pain, how it is acted out, is more important than the underlying pathology. The behavior model suggests that we feel pain because we have learned to feel pain in a particular situation and because the people around us reinforce us in such a way that we continue to feel the pain. For instance, if a child drops a can of soup on her toe, the people around her may react in many different ways. (1) They can let her cry and pay no attention to her; (2) they can scoop her up, pack her into the car, and, while she screams with fear and anxiety, rush her to the Emergency Department of the local hospital as they promise her candy if she stops crying; (3) they can hold her while she cries and attempt to put a cold pack on her toe to relieve the swelling. Their reaction has a great deal to do with her present as well as her future experience of pain. The behavior model begins at the same place as the disease model with (1) observed pain. But instead of focusing on the underlying pathology it (2) tries to identify the pain behavior and how this behavior is reinforced by those around us. All this is for the purpose of (3) changing the behavior and thus the pain.

The disease model has been the common way of trying to understand both acute and chronic pain. But with the advent of dolorology, the study of pain, the disease model is losing ground as a way of explaining and dealing with chronic pain, though it still predominates in explaining acute pain.

It must be made clear that these are attempts at understanding why we feel pain. The present state of knowledge does not allow us to give any absolute answers. We know we hurt. We know that we can do something about that hurt, yet we still find much argument as to why we feel this hurt.

What Can Be Done about Pain

Although we cannot be absolutely certain as to what pain is or what causes it, we know pain exists. It hurts, and we want to do something about it. History is filled with accounts of chemical, surgical, and psychological methods of diminishing pain.

Pills, liquids, injections are all forms of the first, the medical *ingestion of chemicals*. Aspirins for headache pain and medicine for coughs are chemicals that treat the symptoms and possibly the cause of pain. In any case, they often reduce pain.

Surgical procedures are part of our race's memory. Some

skeletons found in ancient Aztec ruins reflect a high degree of knowledge of pain relief through surgery. The most extreme case of the use of surgery for pain is modern psychosurgery. Psychosurgery is surgery performed on an intact brain in order to bring about psychological changes that in turn will change behavior (e.g., smashing one's head against the wall) or relieve tensions and anxieties. It is to be distinguished from brain surgery, which is usually done to correct a known organic condition such as a tumor. With the advances of modern medicine and technology, surgery has become a highly precise science.

An example of this technology is what has come to be called the dorsal column stimulator (D.C.S.), which combines technology and medicine. It is a small device implanted in the spine of a person suffering from an excruciatingly painful disorder such as cancer or spinal-disk disease. The device is relatively simple in design, consisting of a plastic strip not much bigger than a Band-Aid, which contains tiny electrodes attached to a miniature radio receiver. During a brief operation, the D.C.S. is implanted in the skin, just over the spinal cord, with the source of pain determining its position. For example, if the patient suffers from leg pain, the D.C.S. is implanted just above the point at which the nerves from the leg reach the spinal column. When the patient feels a sudden twinge, he or she holds a tiny antenna over the D.C.S.; it relays signals to a small battery-powered transmitter that most patients wear on their belts, and directs a volley of electric impulses into the spine. These impulses abolish the pain signals; the only sensation remaining is a not-unpleasant tingling. These devices provide some relief in 80% of acute pain cases and 25% of chronic pain cases.

Psychological methods run the gamut from biofeedback and hypnosis to conditioning techniques used in many pain centers.

The treatment at the pain center often begins with a lecture. Patients are told that the staff at the center does not believe that pain is a physical handicap. They are also informed of one of the center's strict rules: Patients are not allowed to talk about their pain except during consultations with their doctors, and then only to say if they feel better, worse, or the same. The goal of this strategy is obvious: to end any psychological benefit the person might derive from being able to talk about pain.

Other important parts of the treatment include several hours of instruction, use of electrical pain relievers, vigorous body massages, biofeedback training, and, in some cases, acupuncture.

The success rate is low in the pain centers, but one must remember that those who come to such a center are persons who have had no success with the other methods.

As is evident, there are many technologies that aim at diminishing pain. Some of these really do diminish or eliminate our pain; some do not. But one thing is clear for anyone who has suffered deeply: Whether the pain is eliminated, diminished, or whether it remains as it was, life will never be the same. Physical suffering changes us. Even if we are fortunate enough to have our pain reduced, we are different as a result of the suffering experience. The surgery, the chemicals, the psychological modification, the pain itself are now part of us. We face new choices and new values as a consequence of the suffering situation.

Hospitals, Doctors, and Pain

For many centuries there have been special places and people dedicated to caring for the sick and confronting pain. This was not their only task, nor were caring for the sick and reducing pain always intimately connected. Today both hospitals (our special places) and doctors (our special people) have a role in society and in individual lives they have never before enjoyed. The importance of both the position and the person is shown by the willingness of society to crown them with status and economic well-being. It is obvious that medicine in all its forms is so honored in our society.

We hold doctors in esteem because they deal with something we value: a life without pain. To obtain that life we place them in a position formerly held only by kings and bishops.

Ernest Becker, in his *Denial of Death* (New York: The Free Press, 1973), suggests that as we remove God from heaven and destroy him as a transcendent reality, we put other people and things in God's place. We must do this, says Becker, because we need our god(s) if we are to live. For many, the doctor is God. He or she is all-knowing, all-seeing, all-powerful. The doctor gives life and takes it away. This function of giving and taking has been emphasized to me over and over again in counseling the bereaved. The doctor or the nursing staff is blamed for failing to keep the person alive. A famous surgeon is remembered for those "he lost" as well as for those "he saved." His "losing" them is an indication that people feel he somehow had control of their "wandering away." Somehow he or she made a mistake in diagnosis or lacked the skill to save the individual. The presupposition many have is that we could live forever if we had the knowledge.

In the nineteenth century the physician guided the person into this world at birth and announced to him or her the nearness of death. But today we tend to think of the physician as a god who will enable us to live forever.

It is necessary to realize that the doctor is not God. This is easy to say. We may nod our head in agreement: "Yes, the physician is just a human being," we may think. "Yes, he or she may be on drugs or concerned with family matters while dealing with me." "Yes, he or she may find me sexually attractive and be responding to me as a possible sex partner rather than as one in need of medical help." We can give mental assent to other possible scenarios, but when we come in pain to a doctor, we may blank them from our consciousness. We expect to be cured, or at the very least be offered the hope of a better life. We want him or her to be God. We want doctors to be incapable of making a mistake. The continued and frequent malpractice suits indicate that we expect doctors to be all-knowing and all-powerful like God.

If we do reject their "godliness," if we seriously accept their human fallibility, certain consequences follow: We should always keep track of what and why they do things to us; we should never give them the total responsibility for our lives but instead reserve for ourselves that awesome duty. More specifically, (1) we must make them state clearly what they think is wrong with us. At the same time we must be willing to accept the fact that they may not know precisely what is wrong; they may be making an educated guess. Moreover, we cannot expect simple answers to a possibly complex situation. (2) We must understand what procedures they will use to obtain a more exact diagnosis, cure, or care for the ailment. This may require us to write down the steps and to ask for clarification when we do not clearly understand everything. (3) We must monitor how these procedures are carried out. In a hospital this means, for example, being aware of what drugs we are given and their possible effects upon us. It may mean we refuse treatment until it is clear that what the medical staff is doing is for our betterment and is not just testing or trying some procedure out on us. The individual nurse or doctor may be making a mistake, doing something without the direct request of the doctor in charge, or perhaps mistaking us for another patient. We have all heard stories of such medical mistakes. To lessen the chance of this happening to us, we must be willing to ask questions and sometimes be treated unkindly for asking.

Yet we have to be tactful in exercising our responsibility. We do, after all, need the doctor and other staff members. And we must remember that since pain often makes us feel confused, angry, or guilty, in that state we are apt to say and do things we will regret.

On the other hand, we should keep in mind that the medical people need us. (No patients, no job.) Moreover, they are not used to having patients demand their rights, so it is understandable that they may become confused, angry, even vindictive when we question their conduct.

In short, then, we need to be patient and understanding both with ourselves and with the medical personnel, but we must gently and firmly insist on our rights.

Most hospitals do have what is called a Patient's Bill of Rights. Copies are usually obtained by asking for them. Although they differ from hospital to hospital, they generally include some of the things I have already mentioned. But in spite of the printed Bill of Rights, medical people often have unspoken expectations that the patient will be a passive individual who puts his or her life and health completely into the hands of professionals to do whatever the professionals think is necessary.

We must realize that as medicine has become more specialized, less attention is paid to the human being in the bed and more to the charts and the patient's file. We are the only ones who can be sure it is a person who is being treated, not just an organ or part of the body. This is not an easy task, yet it has to be done if we wish to accept and deal with the total dimensions of suffering and its consequences.

A Painless World: An Empty Promise

Many of us are willing to pay anything to be without pain. We honor the entire health system with status and monetary reward so that we will be free of pain. But all the money and honor will not produce a painless world. Believing in a promise of a painless world is destructive of the world of the present.

We do not like to confront pain. We do not like what it does to us as it jolts us out of our everydayness, changes us, and isolates us from the people, things, and places we love. So we want to avoid pain.

But what would our world be without pain? Some people are actually insensitive to pain. The *New York Times Magazine* (January 30, 1977) told the story of a Miss C., daughter of an Alberta, Canada, physician who was so immune to pain that it endangered her life, exposed her to sprains, infections, even broken bones. As a student at McGill University in the 1950s, she astonished experts at the Montreal Neurological Institute who found that experiments that would have been torture to anyone else—electric shocks, sticks thrust up her nose, needles inserted into her body—caused her no pain at all. Then on August 28, 1955, she was admitted to the University Hospital in Edmonton, suffering from massive infection. For the first time in her life, she actually felt pain and was given pain depressants. She died two days later, at twenty-nine. An autopsy showed a normal brain and nervous system. Here was someone who lived in a world without pain.

A world without pain is beyond the imagination of most of us. It is certainly a different world from the one we know. We want this world without pain, but as the story makes clear, it would not be a better world, just a different one.

Running from Pain

To run from a confrontation with pain is to run from our humanity. To run away from pain in others or self is to run away from that which calls attention to the very body that we are. If pain does anything, it makes us all too aware of that aspect of ourselves that is limited, hurts, and dies.

If avoiding pain is our ultimate value, the most important thing in our life, we destroy all that is good in the present for an empty future. We reject the body and all the body implies. We avoid pain and pain-filled people. In doing so we reject such basic values as love, empathy, and camaraderie.

The total flight from pain is foolish because it is so destructive. Pain is both good and bad. The goodness and badness depend on a context. There is more to pain than a measurement on a machine or a dot on the graph. It is the pain of a human and must be seen in a context beyond the physical.

We can make the total elimination of pain our pivotal value, the focus of our entire world. We can spend our whole life trying to avoid pain. But to deny pain is to deny our humanity, and to deny that is to fall into a hidden pit of desperation, dependence, and despair. Avoiding pain becomes then our religion—negative religion, but a religion nonetheless. Such religion leads to desperation because we cannot avoid pain, to dependence because we soon become dependent upon those people, technologies, and faiths that promise a painless life, and finally to despair because sooner or later we must face pain again and again and again.

To deny pain is also to deny our body, which is a sacred and necessary manifestation of our humanity. It is sacred because it is us. It is to be honored, not avoided. In attempting to run from all pain, we begin to split ourselves off from our body. We become an abstraction. In doing so, we open the doors to such physical neglect and communal dishonoring of the body as we have seen in Hitler's ovens and continue to see in the insensitivity of our culture to those suffering intense physical pain. Physical suffering, which we call pain, is always present even if with the wave of the magician's wand we wish to make it disappear. "Now you see it, now you don't." Impossible!

Conclusion

Each of us hears the singers and the songs of physical suffering in a context of past and present suffering. We have sung and shared at least one of these songs. Many times as we read this chapter we may have thought: "Oh, that's just like So-and-so. . . ." Yet when we hear the song of another person, one of the most difficult things to do is not to say such a phrase and to listen with complete attention. This "listening" is done by hearing the words and the feeling behind them, by seeing the other person's response to pain and the suffering pain causes, by asking questions that are sensitive to the sufferer's situation. The singer will gradually learn, if we listen well, that we appreciate his or her song, that we really *hear* him or her.

What we hear may be difficult to discern. Our reflections on the language of pain and its possible interpretation indicate how complex a task discernment is. This difficulty in understanding these descriptive categories suggests that suffering is a mystery.

Although we may, and must, try to hear the singer and his or her songs, we will never hear nor totally understand these songs exactly as they are sung, for there is a dimension to human beings that is mysterious and goes beyond empirical knowledge.

We can, however, help the sufferer. This chapter indicated some of the means of dealing with physical suffering. Although we concentrated on the physical means to reduce suffering, we hope that every means possible will be used to alleviate it. In addition to the chemical, the surgical, and psychological means, we must include emotional outreach and community support for the sufferer. In other words, we must deal with the whole person.

* * *

Questions for Individual Reflection
1. Divide your life into seven-year periods. What was the greatest physical problem of each period?
2. What is the worst thing that could happen to your body? Become blind? Lame? What?
3. Do you love your body? Yourself?
4. State two things you can do to improve your physical self.
5. For one week do those two things once a day; or if you cannot do them once a day, do them once a week for a month.

Questions for Group Reflection
1. What illness do you think causes the most pain?
2. When did you last visit the doctor? Were you afraid? How did he or she treat you?
3. Do you favor any one method of alleviating pain more than another? Explain.
4. How can we diminish pain yet face up to it?

CHAPTER TWO

Songs of Our Emotions: Emotional Suffering

Singers

"What's life? Birth, death. Everything in between is a drag."

—*Lou Grant on*
"Mary Tyler Moore Show"

"And she began to write on the pad:
  "I must learn to: open bottles, move the furniture, open stuck windows, go home alone, investigate the noise in the night, eat alone, make decisions alone, handle money alone, go on trips alone, fight with service companies alone, be sick alone, sleep alone, sing alone."

—*Adapted from Sonja O'Sullivan's*
"Single Life in a Double Bed,"
Harpers, *November 1975*

" 'He swallowed it!' she cried. For two weeks the young nurse had tried to help the old man, and today he swallowed it. She was so happy. As a patient on her floor he had alienated everyone; in return he was avoided. She thought he must be lonely and tried to help. And he swallowed the water!"

—*Story told to N. Kollar*

"Health studies show that single, widowed, and divorced people are a far likelier prey to disease than the married. Some examples: the coronary death rate among widows between 25 and 35 is five times that of married women in the same age group. At all ages, the divorced are twice as likely as the married to develop lung cancer or suffer a stroke. Among divorced white males, cirrhosis of the liver is seven times more common, and tuberculosis ten times more common."

—Time, *September 5, 1977*

* * *

The singers of songs such as these may be found in any imaginable circumstance: a man leading a life of ease and pleasure that becomes meaningless and thus causes suffering; a young teenager crying because the girl he wanted to date refused him; a poor South American peasant numbed by the death of her third child; Miss America ending her reign at the close of the year. Emotional suffering is as diverse as the human race and as intense as the unique personality of each of its members. In such diversity of singers, however, there are some consistent songs.

Songs

Four songs are the loudest when one listens to the singers of emotional suffering. They can be summarized: "I'm numb"; "I'm afraid"; "Why are they doing this to me?"; "I've got to do something."

1. *"I'm numb."* These singers feel that the world stands still, that they are merely observers of what is happening. They have a difficult time realizing that they are suffering in ways other than this feeling of numbness and of distance from everything and everyone around them. Denial and depression accompany such numbness. Denial is usually defined as an unconscious defense mechanism whereby the truth of certain thoughts, feelings, or wishes is disavowed because the truth is painful or threatening. It is in the context of that definition that the word is used here to indicate a refusal to recognize the reality or the possibility of suffering. This refusal in turn may cause suffering to oneself and to others. When we ask, knowing full well that the person is afflicted with a significant cause of suffering, "Are you okay?" and the response is "Who, me? Of course," we may, if the person thinks he or she is telling the truth, be hearing denial. Or notice the way we easily deny the bodily changes resulting from overeating. We buy a larger size of clothing. When we huff and puff up the stairs, we say we are getting old, instead of looking at the scale. We refuse to let the real reason surface. Such a pattern of denial is merely old-fashioned lying to ourselves, and it numbs us to life.

Depression is commonly found among those who suffer intensely. What is depression? The word itself is certainly familiar. Most of us, at some point in our lives, have described ourselves as depressed. But one type of depression is quite different from the mood we experience so often. Normal depression tells us that we are human, that something is not quite right. It is adaptive: It alerts us to be more responsive to what is going on in our life and to try to change it. It is passing, and does not prevent us from dealing with others, our work, or caring for ourselves.

But intense depression, which is not "normal," is a feeling that is persistent, pervasive, and impairs functioning. Some of the typical symptoms of this type of depression are: sleep disorders—sleeping too much or not enough; self-recrimination—continual re-telling of one's mistakes; being sad, feeling terrible, and having little motivation to do anything; barely moving, not having enough physical energy to walk to the table to eat; having no sex drive; feeling worthless. These are some of the signs of intense or severe depression—signs which, if not responded to, may end in suicide.

2. *"I'm afraid."* Fear is a matrix of emotional suffering. As we look at suffering we find various fears. Fear of the unknown, for example, means that we do not know what is going to happen to us. "What is going to happen to my life? To my family? To my body?" Fear of the unknown now makes all those intimate questions to which we had answers become unanswerable. We are afraid because all our assurances of life have been destroyed.

The fear of being left alone causes suffering. Loneliness is one of the major causes of emotional suffering. It is one thing to choose to be alone; it is quite another to be left alone. The fear of losing our identity is another cause of suffering. We need family and friends to tell us who we were. We need our body and its structure, along with control of that body, to give us a sense of responsibility and adulthood. Anything that causes us to fear the loss of any of these—family, friends, body, self-control—is a source of emotional suffering.

3. *"Why are they doing this to me?"* Much suffering is caused by the feeling that others are the source of what is happening to me and that I am helpless to do anything about it. It is not by chance, I think, that I suffer: Someone else must be responsible for my cancer, my lost job, my child's failure, my boredom. This is expressed many times in anger: "Why me?" "Why did I break my leg, get caught taking the money, or develop this personality?" Sometimes the anger is inarticulate because it knows no object. It wells up inside oneself, trying to break through the oppression that causes suffering, and thus it intensifies the suffering.

4. *"I've got to do something."* Even when we are secure in thinking

we know the reason for our suffering, we may still suffer in trying to find ways to lessen it. The suffering may come in having to travel to other medical centers to find the cure of an ailment; in making regular trips to the hospital or the psychiatrist; in giving large amounts of money to the poor so as to share our goods with the less fortunate; or in writing letters to those in power and participating in demonstrations for human rights.

Bargaining is one way of doing something about suffering. Unfortunately, it often becomes a source of suffering for oneself or others. Bargaining is a strange type of barter, since it is a mixture of exchange and denial. We admit, for instance, that we feel depressed or lonely. The real reason, perhaps, may be the way our job restricts movement and communication, but we say and feel instead that it is our house: "When I get out of this house, I know I'll feel better." Or "It's the weather that makes me depressed and angry. Let's go for a vacation." "If I go to bed, that'll fix me up." A certain willingness to barter is evident when we think that if we change houses, if we go to sleep earlier, if we go on a vacation—if we do this or that, then our suffering will disappear. Sometimes the bargaining works and we feel more reconciled to our life. But sometimes our life is an endless series of bargains as we attempt to end the suffering, only to find that the bargaining itself is a source of suffering.

The Language of Emotional Suffering

Emotions such as the ones found in these songs have a significant role in increasing or decreasing suffering. This role became quite clear to Dr. H. K. Becker while he was serving in a field hospital in Anzio, Italy, during World War II. He noticed that the wounded soldiers, who by all rights should have been begging for relief of their pain, adamantly refused all pain medication. They were so euphoric at simply having survived that their joy blocked out their pain. This experience led Dr. Becker to begin researching the relationship between emotions, pain, and suffering. As a consequence of his and others' research, the relationship between emotions and physical pain is being reexamined. This research is discovering an intimate relationship between emotions, feelings of pain, and the reaction to our pain by others.

The scientists supporting such a holistic approach to life agree that we are more than an arrangement of organs and limbs and that suffering results from more than physical pain alone. The nineteenth-century model of pain is simply not true. The scientists at that time suggested that there were pain nerves, like telephone wires, connected to a switchboard mechanism in the brain. Stimulate these nerves by banging an elbow or burning a finger, and the brain automatically relays back signals that are felt as pain. Feelings, in that view, are nothing more than feelings; they are insignificant in evaluating suffering.

From a holistic perspective, however, emotions are part of every suffering situation. The feeling of loss in a suffering situation is the basic emotion from which the others flow. So a knowledge of the language of loss can open our minds to a deeper understanding of suffering.

We should always remember that the loss that suffering focuses on is never trivial in our songs nor in life generally, for the root loss that is the source of suffering is the loss of self. When we suffer because we have lost someone through death, lost a job, or lost the respect of others, we have actually lost a part of our self. This can be understood by reflecting on how our concept of our "self" depends on more than the image we see in the mirror.

Our self-image is dependent upon our body, other individuals, things, and society as a whole. We see ourselves to a great extent as others see us. For instance, if people ran away from us every time we walked out the door, we would wonder what was wrong and would soon develop a bad self-image. We see ourselves, too, in the way we relate to things. Suppose we like watermelon. One aspect of ourselves is that we are "someone who likes watermelon." Maybe we are good at growing flowers; that is also part of who we are and how we see ourselves. Again, we would have a bad self-image if nothing we did with things worked: Start the car and it falls apart; open the door and we walk away with the handle; turn on the stove and it refuses to light. Our self-image would be challenged, to put it mildly. So everyone and everything we have a relationship with helps create our very selves and the way we see ourselves.

Consequently when we lose something or someone we have established a relationship with, we also lose a part of ourselves. To lose a "non-bodily part" can be as significant as losing a part of our body. To lose a person, a social position, the ability to ride a horse, a deeply held value such as obeying everyone in authority—any of these can be as significant and as painful as losing an arm, leg, or eye. On the other hand, like the men at Anzio, we sometimes feel no pain of loss when we realize that we have not lost that all-important aspect of ourselves, our life.

The Language of Loss

In attempting to be accurate, professionals begin to use terms in an agreed-upon fashion. Hence a vocabulary to describe loss has developed in much the same way as the one to describe pain. Some important terms used to discuss loss are bereavement, grief, and mourning. *Bereavement* is a state of deprivation, whether we feel it or not. *Grief* refers to the feeling of loss and all the emotions that surround such a feeling. *Mourning* refers to the psychological process or pattern through which we express our grief. It is possible that we are bereaved but have no grief and consequently do not mourn. Such distinctions help us realize that not every bereavement or deprivation results in feelings of loss or suffering even if others may expect us to have such feelings. Our concern here, however, is with the suffering brought on by grief. Let us first look at the patterns of grief as found in the mourning process and then at some of the emotions associated with grief.

Mourning

The story of Mr. Green allows us to focus upon the psychological process by which we deal with grief.

When I arrived home from work one day, there was more commotion than usual among the greeting party. As soon as I parked the car the house exploded! From the front door ran my oldest son; from the garage, my wife and two other children.

"Mr. Green's gone!" the four-year-old shouted. "Green gone!" said the two-year-old. The baby just wiggled.

Thank God my wife was there to interpret.

"Rudy lost the doll he calls Mr. Green while we were out walking. Would you mind driving while we look for it on the side of the road?"

So everyone got in, and we began to search for Mr. Green. A clump of grass. An old bottle. A discarded box. All were Mr. Green to various members of the search party. We stopped, started, searched all over again. Cries of

"Here he is!" "There he is!" were heard every few minutes. But we never found him that day. And Rudy cried because he'd lost Mr. Green. We agreed that it was useless to look for the doll. It was lost and we should comfort Rudy over his loss.

The next evening my wife and I admitted that we had gone out of our way to look for Mr. Green. Our son wanted to look again, and we did; no success. We even looked around the house, an action that contradicted the fact that Rudy had actually taken him on a walk. We didn't want to believe that Mr. Green was lost. We felt we *had* to find him. But Mr. Green was *lost*.

Two months later we could see Rudy swinging on his swing with a distant look in his eye, wondering about Mr. Green. And so did we. We all spoke of what might have happened, who might have found him. We wanted some-one to find him. We didn't want to accept the fact that he was lost. But gradually we told our stories enough that both the storyteller and the hearers felt better.

Whether the sufferer is my son losing his Mr. Green or any one of us losing a dear friend, our way of mourning the loss shows a common threefold pattern of response: (1) alarm, (2) denial-protest-search, and (3) resignation. Sometimes we become conscious of these feelings in the order just given. At other times they seem a jumble that leaves us drained of energy and vitality. Perhaps we don't experience the loss as intensely when we lose a twenty-dollar bill as when we lose a job, but our emotional pattern of response to the loss is basically the same since these are some ways we deal with any felt loss.

1. *Alarm.* When we first discover the loss we are shocked. We might scream, faint, curse, swear, sweat. From the depths of the unconscious we react to fight off this evil. We lash out either ver-bally or nonverbally, trying to rid ourselves of the feelings caused by this loss. Our mouth is dry; we feel helpless, perhaps dizzy. What is happening is that we are sustaining the initial shock of never being the same again. This experience may occur when we discover we are seriously ill, when we realize that the divorce will happen, when we are conscious that we are living an empty life. When we first realize that what was is no more, our entire organism reacts to this threat of disintegration. But even while the alarm or shock reaction sets in we are beginning the

restorative process found in denial, protest, and search.

2. *Denial-Protest-Search.* It is difficult to accept the fact that something or someone is gone forever and that as a consequence of this loss, we will never be the same again. We say "It's not really gone." As with Mr. Green, we look everywhere trying to find what has been lost. Our ride to find Mr. Green days after we were mentally convinced we had lost him was much like a protest march in which we were saying both "No, he's not lost" and at the same time "No, he shouldn't be gone!" We deny and protest and at the same time search. We think we have found what we lost: A stranger's profile reminds us of the person who is dead; a voice sounds like his or her voice; or, as with Mr. Green, even when we got out of the car and walked up to the bottle we imagined was Mr. Green, we had to pick it up before we could throw it away, saying: "It's not Mr. Green." We actually had to touch the object.

We protest what is lost, perhaps by becoming bitter about what has occurred. The alarm reaction to severe loss turns us in upon ourselves. When a person only looks at himself or herself, it is natural to see this as the only world, to feel that this is the only loss. "No one else has ever gone through what I'm going through," we protest. Feelings like this lead to bitterness and anger. We strike out at those around us. This is a very irrational reaction, but suffering is irrational, so it is foolish to expect rational behavior in such a situation. We usually feel guilty in addition to being angry: guilty for not having cared enough, for not having spent enough time together, for not having enjoyed the one lost while he or she was present. Thus guilt, along with anger, is part of the denial-protest-search movement.

Denial-protest-search usually does not last a long time; it is cause for great concern if it does. But what is a long time? It varies greatly with the individual and with the situation; there is no rigid norm or perfect pattern. For people who have been married for many years and have had a deep love relationship, three years is not unusual. For other losses, such as a job, the pattern of denial-protest-search is over almost as soon as the losses are replaced. What we do know is that the healing, the restorative process, does take time. Gradually we withdraw from what we loved so much and lost; we move on to new and perhaps deeper levels of meaning and love, to new ways of living.

Why do we keep going in the face of loss? Why does the mourning process continue when to all intents and purposes, especially in severe loss, the person may feel no reason to continue living? People give many reasons for continuing to live and face their loss, some more important than others: duty, God's will, friends, joy, children, finances, self-image. But ultimately we search because we realize we must survive. Many things and people help us recognize that we must survive. They pull us beyond the shock of discovery and beyond the process of denial-protest-search. Somewhere along the line we say, "That's it! I can't keep going this way," and we work our way through the grief associated with loss.

The mourning process and grief are difficult, tiring work. They are not done in a moment or a day. Getting over loss is like getting over a physical wound: It takes time. But it is worthwhile. When it heals there is still a mark of what happened, but often we are stronger than before. Working through loss leads to a new life, one that is certainly different and sometimes better than the one we have lost. While we are caught in mourning and grief, it seems as though the new life will never come. But it will. The experience of the human race demonstrates this truth, though it is difficult to believe in the midst of our loss.

3. *Resignation* is the state we reach when mourning has ended but the memory of our loss continues. We have a fond memory of the one lost, but it is a feeling tempered by reality. We remember the good and the bad. We may, in the remembering, feel a wave of grief that will be described later. For we never forget those we love dearly. But we do gain a new perspective of living without the one we remember. We are willing to try again, to invest ourselves again. With renewed investment in life, the mourning process ends but the memory remains.

Grief

Grief is the word generally used to refer to the emotional response to loss. Grief, however, is difficult to describe. For those who have experienced it, no explanation is necessary; for those who have not, no explanation is possible. Basically it is how we feel when we lose something or someone. This feeling is both a conglomerate of other feelings and a concentration of the feeling of loss itself. Let me first describe the concentrated feeling of grief that I call "a wave of grief."

A wave of grief occurs when we become aware of the deep emptiness in ourselves resulting from a loss. Many mixed emotions crowd into us at these moments: misery, despair, sorrow, emptiness, loneliness, disbelief, distance from others, yearning for what is lost. All these feelings usually result in the physical reactions of crying, taking deep breaths, and feeling weak. This mixture of feelings and physical reactions is called waves because, like waves along the seashore, they come with varied frequency and power. They are usually intense during the first weeks of loss but lessen as we put more time between us and the loss.

The best way to deal with waves of grief is not to deal with them: Let them happen, and they will pass. In many ways it is similar to feeling sick to our stomach. There is a buildup, buildup; then it all comes out and we feel a little better, though weaker. Waves of grief are the same: the building up of each wave in its individual intensity; sobs, empty feeling, memory of the one lost, wishing he or she were present. Then it is over, until the next wave. Any attempt to stop this process over a prolonged period of time results in psychosomatic reactions in the person.

The conglomerate of feelings surrounding loss (as distinguished from the concentrated feeling of grief that we have been discussing) is a mixture of underlying reactions experienced by persons who have lost someone or something. Few people experience all these reactions; most feel some of them. We will look at a few of the common ones.

It is not unusual to have varied *dreams* of what is lost. It is not unusual, either, to repeat over and over again how it was lost. We seem driven to repeat the story. People may think we are crazy, but this repetition is actually a way we deepen the realization of loss while preparing to live again.

Those who have taken care of someone for a long time often feel *relief*. When the person dies, the caregiver suddenly feels relieved that it is all over. This is mentioned here because sometimes people will hesitate to admit such a feeling, or if we hear someone say it we might think he or she is mean or selfish. Quite the contrary. The person is expressing a natural response to the loss of someone he or she may have taken care of for many years. Such persons cared because they loved. But the care was also a process of suffering for them, so a feeling of relief at the end of such a difficult endeavor may be expected.

Another common reaction is to *substitute other things* for what we have lost. In the loss of a part of the body, this usually takes the form of some prosthetic device. When we lose a person in death, divorce, or permanent dislocation, the substitution takes other forms: a picture, a favorite object of the person, a place, even an animal.

Physical reactions: We may either lose or gain weight, depending upon how we use food in a crisis situation. Loss of balance is not uncommon in severe grief situations; nor is illness or even death. The stories of the deaths of widows or widowers demonstrate this.

Loss and Gain

We can all look back to significant losses and gains. We have undergone significant changes. If we look, for instance, at the changes that happened between pre-puberty and puberty, we see significant losses and gains. We lose dependence upon parents; we lose treating the opposite sex without genital attraction; we lose freedom in the midst of security. We gain a new sensual attraction to the opposite sex; we gain a broader range of choices and movement, ranging from wider educational opportunity to getting our first driver's license. In totaling up the losses and gains it is often difficult to know what is really a loss or really a gain and which set outweighs the other.

At each stage of our life it is of course impossible to look down life's road and foresee what life will be like. What is a loss to us now may well become an advantage later on. I know someone who, because he had attended a very inadequate grammar school, had never learned to spell or write properly. Because of his inadequacies, he had to work twice as hard as the other students in his high school. The result was that by the twelfth grade he was a superior student. What started out as a loss ended up as a gain. This type of "positive loss" is often evident as we look back at our lives.

However, certain losses can destroy the personality. To lose a job, a spouse, a child, an education, a part of the body—each of these may be devastating.

Yet when we think about it, there is nothing we can claim as absolute loss, a loss that we can be absolutely sure will destroy us forever; even death itself is conquered by immortality. (*Hell* is the word we use to symbolize absolute loss.) We all know stories of how loss has been turned into gain even while mourning the loss. "Make Today Count," a volunteer organization of cancer patients and their families, began because a man was convinced that in facing a life-destroying cancer it is best to concentrate on life rather than death. He wanted to make every day count. I always remember an evening in St. John, New Brunswick, Canada. My wife and I were assigning rooms for guests at a national Newman convention. A bubbly young girl came to the desk, signed the register, took her key, and went to her room. Something about her appearance caught my eye, but I couldn't figure out what it was. The next morning at breakfast she happened to be at the table we were sharing. I then realized what was unusual about her: She had no arms. But there she sat, eating with her feet in an easy, carefree manner. We learned that she had been born this way and that her parents were convinced she must not be babied because of her loss. In the midst of their suffering over what had happened to their daughter, they concentrated on what to do for her, not for themselves. For this love we were thankful, for her loss was our gain as we witnessed her joyful life.

Everything that happens to us has this twofold character to it. There is no such thing as pure loss, absolute evil, in this world, just as there is no such thing as pure gain or absolute good. As long as the occurrence is a human occurrence, its evaluation depends upon the context. It waits for the outcome for its final evaluation. The whole song must be sung before we know what it is.

Loss and gain can be judged only according to the norm of life itself. Life, whether of the individual or of humanity, awaits its last breath before being judged. And any final judgment must await the final breath of life. It is obvious that there cannot be a world without loss. If such a world existed, we would have no growth: To walk, for instance, a man must "lose" where he was in order to "gain" where he will be. This is true for anyone who wishes to be human.

The feelings associated with loss will always be with us because loss is always with us. This is to say something we already know: that suffering is part of life. But seeing loss as an essential aspect of life lets us see suffering from another angle.

As we look at the loss of self-image, we are at each stage of life faced with what to do about that loss. Each stage faces us with the need to accept deep loss (to our self-image) as well as minor losses (our own Mr. Green). To accept loss too quickly is to play the coward; to deny the reality of loss is to be an idiot. How does one learn to deal with loss? When should one hold on? When should one let go?

Practical Suggestions for Coping with Loss

The language of loss shows us searching, hoping to find our Mr. Green. Our task in coping with loss is twofold: to realize whether finding is possible or impossible, and to act accordingly.

Is it realistic to search for what is lost? When we ask such a question, we must realize that two important factors are involved: our relationship to the loss, which involves many and varied feelings, and the hard evidence of what is not there anymore. For example, to lose a job may cause us to *feel* that we have lost status in the community and that our self-worth has been lessened. But it may also mean that we have lost food, clothes, money in the bank. The feelings have to be dealt with because they are real. At the same time, though, we must search for the hard evidence of what is (or is not) there any more. We must ask: Have we really lost the thing in question? Is the loss permanent? Let us look at both dimensions—the feelings and the hard evidence.

Feelings

Feelings are vague. It takes much reflection, anguish, and talking to make them specific. The following may aid in clarifying your feelings.

1. Feel the feeling. Ride it like a wave of water. Get to know its direction, its source, its specialness. If you can do so, make notes about how you feel. Characterize it. Draw it.

2. Talk with someone you feel relaxed with, someone you trust to accept what seems absurd, because the initial forming of words is most difficult and strange.

3. Ask, What have I lost? Usually there is much more than the object, person, animal, or body part. Can you do without it? Do not be afraid to grieve for it.

Hard Evidence

Hard evidence about what is lost can only be obtained by actually reviewing the evidence. Call those involved in any decision causing the loss, such as the doctor, the analyst, the governmental agency. Read literature about the loss (e.g., an illness). Talk to the experts. Ask questions. If you investigate, a time will come when the evidence shines forth as to whether there has been a real loss and whether the loss is permanent. Strangely enough, the empirical evidence of loss is quite similar to evidence about the emotional side. It is not solid and incontrovertible. Instead, it ebbs and flows according to our acceptance or non-acceptance of the reality that what we had will be ours no more.

We may come to accept loss intellectually but not emotionally. This is not unusual; it takes time for one's whole self to accept a significant loss. So it is nothing to worry about. Our own awareness of loss is basically a willingness to deal with what has happened. Only time and love will fill the emptiness that remains when we lose someone or something.

Perhaps you are not grieving but are in a position to help those who are. Over the years, I have developed a list of dos and don'ts for helping such people. An awareness of these dos and don'ts can help you deal with your own grief as well. (Remember that these suggestions are designed for those who have suffered severe loss.)

Don'ts

1. Don't probe. Wait until the person in some way invites you to talk with him or her. Be present, but don't harass. This demands that you be at ease with yourself and your purpose in being there, which is to be of service, not to exercise power over the other.
2. Don't be afraid to show your own feelings that are in sympathy with the other's feelings. You should not be afraid of crying or of showing disgust or anger over what has happened.
3. Don't pity the person. Pity turns the other person into an object, puts him or her into an inferior position.
4. Don't be afraid of silence. Silence is a great cure, but you must be willing to live with it. When you are anxious to help and a person is quiet, you may easily think you are useless. Not so! Your quiet presence is a strong guarantee of concern, since you demand neither to give nor to receive. Instead you are sharing the other's suffering.
5. Don't be afraid of embarrassment. For example, don't be afraid of doing or saying the wrong thing (as you may well do). Don't be embarrassed to talk even though it may seem shallow in the face of the loss you are sharing with the person. Go where the other leads, and go with love.
6. Don't be afraid to laugh with one who is grieving. Laughter puts life in perspective.

Dos

1. Prepare well ahead of time if possible. Reading a book such as this one can be a good preparation. To realize that every one of us experiences loss will enable you to deal on an equal basis with a person who is experiencing loss. Empathy and trust are best built before the situation occurs. You must be willing to spend the time necessary to build up such a relationship.

2. Protect the person from intruders in the initial stages of mourning. During shock and bewilderment one is often as helpless as a baby. The initial stages usually occur when the person first discovers the loss, not necessarily when it is ritualized—e.g., not at the funeral but at the notification of death; not at the operation but upon hearing the doctor's diagnosis; sometimes not even upon hearing the diagnosis but later when the full realization of the doctor's words hits home.

3. Stick around and help with day-to-day tasks such as caring for the children and preparing food. In the early stages, make few demands on the grieving person, though this should gradually change as time progresses. Be prepared to deal with the other's tendency to pour out feelings of anguish and anger directed at you. He or she will take out some negative feelings on you.

4. Indicate that he or she does not have to bottle up feelings when you are around; yet allow for the other's privacy. *You* may not be the one this person can best grieve with, and thus you must always be prepared to leave the person alone if he or she wishes it. In our society most people grieve alone.

5. Know what normal grief and mourning are like so you can reassure grievers that everything is normal even if they do not feel it is. Do not repeat this too many times, though, because they may then feel that what they are going through is trivial. There is a happy medium between saying it too often and not saying it at all.

6. Remember: When you are making one person comfortable, you may be making another uncomfortable. Friends or family members often feel threatened, anxious, or restless while attention is focused upon the one who is grieving. Many people are still not comfortable, for instance, in speaking about the dead person years after the funeral.

7. Things take time. Mourning and grief are measured in months and years. Affirm a creative future.

8. Listen.

Conclusion

Behind these dos and don'ts is the holistic image we have stressed throughout this chapter. Each loss influences the way we see ourselves as well as the way we are. Each of us is in a process of change and development. The loss that is most serious is the loss that threatens the self-concept of a person at that particular moment in his or her life. Losing a parent, for instance, when one is six is different from losing a parent when one is married and sixty-six. We must, therefore, be sensitive to the total person who is suffering and to what his or her sense of self is.

This is extremely important in an era when some professionals are advocating "honesty" or "overcoming denial" in a way that forgets the person one is being honest with or being realistic toward. Some people believe that the facts are all that is necessary to help a person through the experience of loss. They believe that we should tell the person straight out what has happened to him or her or what will happen. But what may be a simple statement of truth to the teller may be destructive to the hearer, who hears it in terms of his or her self-concept. We must never forget the singer as we hear and share the songs of suffering.

Suffering affects the whole self. In hearing the songs of emotional suffering, we concentrated on the loss that is present in suffering. In concentrating on such loss, we may have overlooked our reason for hearing such songs. We listen to the loss so that we can help the person toward living a fuller life after the mourning process. We can never replace what is lost, but we can help the person realize that he or she is still important and needed without the valued object or person. The new self that slowly evolves from the seeming void of loss is loved into existence by our hearing the song and sharing the loss. In the dos and don'ts we saw how to do this sharing and hearing. Central to our listening was the conviction that the person must be respected for who he or she is while we listen to his or her song. The presupposition is that there are persons who are willing to share the song of others. The hope is that the readers of this book will be willing to do so.

* * *

Questions for Individual Reflection
1. On whom do you depend? On what do you depend? Do you depend upon someone to blame for what goes wrong?

2. What have been your two most significant losses during the last fourteen years?
3. Have you ever become resigned to those losses?
4. To whom can you talk regarding your losses? Have you done so recently?
5. How many times do you get angry during a typical day? Is the anger focused on any particular person, place, or circumstance?

Questions for Group Reflection
1. Do you know anyone who has gone through any of the emotions associated with loss?
2. What are the most significant happenings in the state of grief? Would you want to add any other happenings?
3. Is it difficult to know what you are feeling about some person or some thing?
4. Who is a good model for dealing with loss?

CHAPTER THREE

Songs of Our Society: Communal Suffering

We the Singers

Sing of Security: *In 1981 the global arms budget of all countries was estimated at $550 billion a year, about $100 billion of which went into nuclear weapons. $550 billion equals the entire annual income of half of this earth's four billion people. Some $7.42 billion was the proposed cut in the 1982 budget for the U.S. Department of Health and Human Services. The approximate cost of one new carrier task force is $10 billion. The explosive power of the 16 missiles on one Poseidon submarine is more than that used by all the munitions in World War II. We have so many weapons that something is going to have to be done with them. We swallow our medicine, eat our food, play with our toys. How will we consume our armaments? We cannot eat them. Will we let them waste away? We will perhaps know in our lifetime. No matter what the future holds, purchasing them causes suffering for millions and a drain on the economy.*

Sing of Food: *"People are eating out more and more." "Frozen specialty foods are big sellers in the supermarket." "Americans eat more meat than any other nation on earth." These are a few of the items found in the daily newspaper. Yet even affluent people are suffering from malnutrition. They are starving because they eat junk foods. A balanced diet is so rare that we need vitamins to supplement our regular meals. We are an overweight people because we have too much food but do not know how to choose the proper food. Yet even though these facts are recognized, we buy more, we allow advertisements to urge us to eat more. Diet fads, heart attacks, poor self-images, obesity, depression are a few of the effects. The hourly jingle to drink and eat is heard over every radio and television.*

Sing of Possessions: *Our Great Lakes are sewers; our rivers are drains for industrial garbage. The air we breathe is polluted. Cancer is on the increase. . . . The story is familiar. The causes are known. The American public "needs" new products. We need a car to go to work, get the groceries, pick up the children. We need plastic bottles and throwaway cans. We need a car so much that we are willing to die of pulmonary disease. We need things so badly that we are willing to die for them. For a job, a person is willing to work in a plant producing toxic chemicals or high radiation. The production and use of so many nonessential things causes physical suffering through disease and causes social suffering by destroying the environment.*

Sing of Pills: *"There are so many pills, so many medicines to manipulate the body and its emotions. There is a pill for everything. Pills are our defense against suffering. They are also a barrier to life. But if we 'solve' our problem by taking a pill, the problem is never solved, only forgotten. If I am angry with someone over the way his or her dog tears up the lawn and I solve the tension by taking a pill to relax, I have run away from the problem. Suppose someone I work with is not carrying his or her load. This forces me to do more to get the job done. To get that job done I take a pill to have more energy for the work. Actually I've run away from the problem. Moreover, our bodies suffer from unknown side effects of pills, society suffers because we avoid the cause by treating the symptoms, and people we love suffer because we meet them in a daze. Our song is not our own; it is found in the pill dispenser."*

—*N. Kollar,* Mapping Suffering

* * *

We know these songs, for we are the singers. These few demonstrate our communal suffering. "Kiss my knee, Mama!" cries the small child. People shout "Jump!" to the young woman poised for a suicide leap. Underpaid migrant workers harvest crops while we push our shopping cart between the aisles of fruits and vegetables complaining about the high prices. An international corporation closes its steel plants in a Midwestern city. All these are examples of how other people, as individuals or as a group, affect a person's suffering.

The Paradox of the Individual Within Community

I am not alone. I need other people, things, and values to be myself. I need to eat, to drink, to breathe. Without these, I die. I need other people to love, to agree with me, to love me. Without these people, I die. I need a reason to live from moment to moment. I need answers to the questions I ask. Without these, I die. I need this community of things, people, and meaning, or I die.

Yet I am not the community; I am a free individual. I am somebody even though I could not live without these people and things. There is something about me that wishes to transcend everything around me, yet I realize I cannot do it. I want to fly like a bird: independent and free. Yet I know I am human. This is the paradox: I need others, yet I want to be free of them; and when I am free of them, I want them.

The word "others" has many levels of meaning. These "others" may be significant others such as mother, father, spouse, friend, or child. These "others" may be a structure or reality such as a nation, industry, or international church. These "others" may be the culture that socializes us by rewarding and punishing the way we speak and act. Each of these "others" produces communities of suffering and must be understood in order to appreciate the songs of suffering.

Significant others involve us in suffering. After all, it is only when we become deeply attached to a spouse, child, or friend that we grieve deeply when we lose that person. The joy and happiness resulting from his or her love easily turns into personal loss when the source of love disappears.

A nation, city, church, way of life, or any special group may also be a source of suffering to us. These institutions affect us directly: for example, favorite ball teams as they win or lose; nations as they dominate or are dominated in world politics; a church when it seems to abandon its values. These groups that we become part of by birth, interest, or chance become almost another self. We ourselves are Number One when they win; we grieve when they lose.

Both the small community of significant others and the larger institutional community are instruments of socialization. From the first moment the crying baby is picked up, others influence his or her suffering. Our cry for help at any age is a cry for another to react to us, to alleviate our suffering. This community surrounding us throughout our life shapes our feeling and our language of pain. For the feelings as well as our reaction to pain and suffering are learned. For instance, the pain of frostbite is unknown to people in the torrid zone. When we of the temperate zone experience this pain there is no way to interpret it to those people. The hunger pains of one on a diet in America and of one who eats once every two days in Mexico are understood differently by the community as well as by the individual. Even in smaller communities this variation in speaking about and experiencing pain is true. Among the community of football players, pain is a part of the job. When everyone cheers the fullback who gets hit hard after running 20 yards, his is one experience of pain. When I get hit just as hard by someone running down the street and I sit there bleeding, alone with my hurt, except for a vagrant who looks worse than I do and my five-year-old daughter who cries because her doll was broken when I fell, this is still another experience of pain. There is no crowd to cheer me, pay me, or even be concerned about my hurt.

In any of these instances, the way the community reacts to the pain determines in large measure our own reaction to it. The community teaches us to disregard some pain, to feel other pain more intensely than we might have felt it on our own. The community also teaches us how to communicate our feeling of pain. Pain is human experience, and so it is molded according to communal models, as is our sense of beauty and danger or our religious experience. What is pain in one community may not be understood as such in another community.

We live with these "others" who are part of many communities at once, just as we are. Each of these communities affects our suffering. Like a puppet at the end of many strings, we react to the pull of these many communities. Through our body course the joys and sorrows resulting from the influence of these communities. We cannot cut the strings, for without these strings we cannot fully exist. But there is a danger in picturing each of us as a puppet and society as puppeteer. For *we* are society; we are both the puller of strings and the pulled.

The story of Job in the Bible is helpful here because of its basic image: the sufferer surrounded by his friends, and each of his friends interpreting Job's suffering for him. This happens often. For instance, after a death, friend after friend speaks his or her understanding of suffering. From the depths of these friends comes the tragic song of their life as they try to comfort the sufferer. Yet in the attempt to comfort the sufferer they can easily cause discomfort. Their words and actions intensify or diminish the suffering according to the sufferer's acceptance of them. It is not unusual for the community to be finished grieving the dead person long before those more deeply involved with him or her have finished. Thus the community diminishes the suffering by sharing it during the first weeks of loss but intensifies it later on when people expect those grieving to act just the way they themselves are acting. Because neither they nor those around them understand the mourning process, sometimes those who are still grieving a year after the death think they are insane. Instead of experiencing normal grief as part of the mourning process, they label and experience it as neurosis because they are not aware of how normal persons react when they grieve. This normal type of suffering is not recognized in the community, and thus the individual has no way to interpret it.

Another example of how a community influences us is found in what we describe as the ordinary way of doing things. "Well, we usually do it this way" is the opening sentence of some members of the family, neighborhood, or culture. These customary ways of doing things are usually a great comfort. They relieve us of the burden of continually making decisions, and they give us support in what we do. Yet the moment may come when we wish to do things differently. We may stop using our car, heating our house, or gossiping. In the area of health, we may elect to use only ordinary means to sustain our life; as a consequence, people think we are odd for not using experimental drugs or risky operations. So we are isolated, alone in our suffering.

Communities of and for the Suffering: Songs of Communal Suffering

Sufferers have recognized their interdependence by banding together in groups such as Widow to Widow, Parents without Partners, and Alcoholics Anonymous. The purpose of communities of sufferers is to gather together those who have a common "type" of suffering so that they can share their problems, their joys, their interests. In doing so, they give tremendous support to one another. Anyone faced with prolonged bouts of suffering should search out those with the same concern. The telephone book, Lifeline, Got a Problem, and many other social agencies can put one in contact with these specialized groups. Initially we may hesitate to participate in such gatherings. But if we overcome this initial hesitation, we find the group can help in many ways: socially, economically, physically. Life becomes much more livable when we step out of a world that refuses to look at our suffering and into a community of fellow sufferers who understand *us* because they are experiencing the same cause of suffering. *Our* life changes because we now live in a context of shared suffering.

For our present purposes, we may speak of two types of communities for the suffering: those who recognize their own suffering and thus attempt to help others, and those who help the suffering but are not aware of their own suffering. A clear example of the latter are many doctors and nurses who see their role in society simply as helping those in need. An example of the former are those same nurses and doctors who recognize that they *participate* in a society of mutual suffering.

We must be aware of the two extremes, however, when we deal with these institutions. On the one hand, they may easily exaggerate their abilities to take away suffering. Like the advertisements on TV that promise health if we take certain medications regularly, many institutions easily promise more than they can deliver. On the other hand, we should not become cynical about these institutions, because they really can do much to help us.

Suffering and Social Structure

Beyond the smaller communities of and for the suffering is society in general. The communities of and for the suffering are sensitive to the individual sufferers and take the means to deal with them. But, as mentioned before, there is a certain dimension of any society that we refer to as "it." This is the structure of society, a structure each of us participates in, that is something other than any member of the society or the sum of its members.

Once we become aware of the social nature of suffering, we can never again claim neutrality: We are both the victim and the executioner. We kiss the child's knee, shout for the woman to jump, buy the food picked by migrants, protest the closing of the plants. We cannot remain neutral. As Martin Luther King, Jr., said: "We will have to repent in this generation not merely for the vitriolic words and actions of the bad people but for the appalling silence of the good people." Once sensitive to suffering, we realize we are both the cause and the victim of suffering. This is a sobering thought. How to understand and cope with that double status has been a constant challenge to people of good will. Some ways to deal with the challenge are: Ignore the suffering caused by society; never participate in anything that causes suffering; share the suffering that comes when we seek to form a just society.

The first way, although attempted by many, only causes more suffering. We ignore suffering at the price of actually increasing it and facing its more intense form later. Because the suffering of native Americans and Blacks was ignored at the Revolution, it returns to haunt us. Denying women the right to vote gave rise to women's present struggle for justice. Because the vast majority of people ignored these injustices, the structure of society itself must be modified if these minorities are to suffer less.

If we attempt to avoid causing any suffering in others (the second way), we are beginning an impossible task and are hoping for an unreal world. We cannot act without causing some suffering, whether or not our action is justifiable. If, for instance, we refuse to use the products of the multinational corporations, both we and their underpaid workers will suffer. If we advance in our job, someone else does not advance; if our child wins a race, other children lose; if we cut a tree for sunshine, our next-door neighbor loses shade. If Americans slow the arms race, people lose jobs; if the feminists dominate the courts and the media, many men and women have to change their life-style. To avoid causing *any* suffering is impossible.

The third way recognizes that suffering will always be with us but seeks to reduce suffering caused by unjust communal structures. This approach makes the most sense. Let us first discuss some of the theory behind this approach and then offer a method for implementing it.

Unjust Communal Structures: A Theory and a Practice

A Theory: Moral Humans, Immoral Society
In 1932 Reinhold Niebuhr wrote a book entitled *Moral Man and Immoral Society* (New York: Charles Scribner's Sons). In it he points out that we do not critique the social structure the same way we critique individual human actions. That is why, he says,

societies act differently from the individuals who compose them. Social structures escape the moral restraints placed on the individual human person. The larger the social group, the more it seems to act as if there were no moral laws.

We see this phenomenon when a football coach encourages his players to hurt and maim another player, and both players and fans feel happy when the person is injured and they "win." We see it when we feel that the only restraint on a nation's waging war is its technological capacity to wage it. We would see it if the industrialized countries should become energy-sufficient and then leave the Middle Eastern nations to return to poverty without a hint that their poor should be cared for.

Reactions such as these are admitted as facts of life today. We know that appeals to reason and conscience are usually ineffective when we deal with groups. So we often use other kinds of force to influence the actions of large groups: economic force, military force, or the force of public opinion. The use of such force recognizes that evil exists in the very fabric of society. This structural evil causes communal suffering and must be dealt with in order to diminish suffering. We cannot cover over this reality by suggesting it is people who are evil, not society. People may indeed be evil, but so may the structure of society. Nor can we cover over this reality by saying that legally constituted authority is of itself good. For laws and the authority they exercise may also be responsible for inhumanity toward humans just as much as a murderer is responsible for the death of another person. Nor can we become cynical in the face of structural evil, saying by our cynicism that suffering caused by injustice is here to stay, so we should accept it. Such fatalism, whether preached by a president or a pope, is nothing more than a plea for the status quo and its injustices.

Whether the immoral structures of society are easy or difficult to discern, they are always difficult to change. I would like now to suggest a method for dealing with those immoral structures – one that came into prominence about fifteen years ago: the action-reflection method. I first used it in the urban training programs in Washington, D.C., though the example I give did not occur there. The method is a simple one. These people began by wishing to aid a parolee. They were not aware of structural evil but quickly become sensitive to the existence of such evils implicit in our prison system and in our unforgiving society. This same method may be used in approaching larger issues of peace and justice.

A Practice: The Action-Reflection Method

The desire to help others is what usually gets people moving. The group of people I knew began with the rather vague desire to help those in prison. The chaplain of the local state penitentiary asked them if they would be sponsors for a man who was up for parole. After much thought and some investigation, they agreed. Then they gathered together fourteen people filled with good will and interested in helping the parolee.

The group's first meeting was frustrating. Everyone wanted to help the parolee in his new life, yet no one knew *what* to do or *how* to go about implementing this desire. So the meeting was long and frustrating. Out of the frustration, however, was born an approach to the problem: We agreed to search for ways to help the parolee and to gather regularly to share our information. The first step was to assign specific areas to investigate: the legal responsibility of sponsors, searching out job placements, finding a place to live, the relationship of the sponsors to the parole officer, the financial needs of the parolee and of the group, methods of dealing with those on parole, a detailed report on the parolee's background.

Everyone scattered after the first meeting, bound together only by the phone lines. Each of us investigated our assigned area, yet our investigation somehow lacked purposefulness. The second meeting, with the parole officer, helped give us a sense of realism and purpose. He defined the task of the group as a whole, as well as the tasks of the individual persons in the group. He also revealed the inner workings of the parole system with all its political dynamics. For the first time the group had a glimpse of the political and social structure of the prison system. Subsequent meetings with the parole officer dealt with specific problems of the parolee and the developing difficulties of the group as it saw the unique structure of the prison system. The action-reflection method helped the group cope with the individual needs of the parolee and with the larger structural evils of the prison system.

Definition of the Method

"Action-reflection" is a process of effecting institutional changes through directed experiences of engagement in social problems and reflection upon that engagement.

The key words in the definition are *institutional changes*. In our example, the group began with the typical Band-Aid approach: A prisoner was about to enter a lonely world and we were trying to provide for his care. We ended with a concern for many individuals and the structures oppressing them. Here are the four steps we took.

Steps in the Method

1. *Exposure.* Exposure consists of data-gathering with the purpose of examining the possibilities for effecting change or for intervening in a situation. Sometimes exposure is also necessary for people to discover how others live. It was helpful for us to have some type of "exposure" to the parolee's situation. But for us to go out and get completely "exposed" would have been both dangerous and nonproductive. Instead we went to the prison, talked with some prisoners, and then were shown what a prisoner had to do to be paroled. We were also "exposed," through a long and detailed discussion with the parole officer, to what the parolee would encounter once he had left the prison.

Data-gathering means more than acquiring the facts; it is an attempt to *experience* the situation as people actually live it. It is an attempt to get into their skin, so to speak, in order to understand the problem as *they* see it. But direct exposure must also include a certain amount of theoretical input that provides the background material for determining realistic goals. This theoretical input helps the group understand the possibilities and limits of social change, including the constraints and convictions of the various groups involved in the change. For example, there were obvious limitations to the parolee's preparation for facing life outside the prison. He could not be trained for the specific job he might get. He could not work part-time outside the prison while spending his nights in prison. An understanding of the structure and monetary situation of the state's prison system made it clear that it was impossible to give the prisoner more preparation without completely restructuring the system. The system itself was responsible for the suffering of this individual.

The combination of actual exposure with professional input prevents those with quick solutions from dominating the decision-making process. Most people begin working out strategies before they complete the necessary analysis. Almost any group that gathers to work on a social problem contains some people with ready-made solutions. The gathering of all available data (written and spoken, practical and theoretical) is an attempt to avoid the easy answer. It is a very difficult step and one that demands great patience and sympathy.

In our situation we changed our goals when we began to realize that the parolee would probably have to return to crime to survive outside the prison. Knowing this specific person who was suffering injustice was important. An exposure to the change-agents (i.e., all those desiring social change) enabled those of us who were sponsoring the parolee to see that we must keep our horizons low and specific. The enormity of the situation was overwhelming as we faced the powers we had to deal with in our respective tasks. The ponderous and fortuitous actions of the state parole board made us face up to the reality of human limitation. The parole board was composed of part-time people appointed by the governor to repay some political debts. Sometimes they met after supper and drinks; sometimes, on a weekend. They seldom had read the information sent to them. We also learned that they were easily swayed by the Warden who, with the wrinkle of a brow, could delay one person's parole as easily as he could encourage them to parole many inmates because of overcrowding. If one was lucky enough to come up for parole on a day when the Warden was feeling well, when the prisons were overcrowded, and when the board was not too tired, one had a good chance to be paroled. The totality of the situation that involved victims, change-agents, various powers (political, religious, economic), and opinions of experts all helped bring our grandiose ideals into the arena of concrete political action. At the same time, being exposed to the many people who made up the parole system enabled us to plan and carry out achievable goals.

2. *Planning.* We were very slow in gathering information because all of us had other responsibilities. We discovered that the parolee needed both a place to live and people who would realistically attempt to reintroduce him into the outside world. Our goal was twofold: to help this one person and, as a result of assisting him, begin to develop a system involving non-professionals in parolee rehabilitation.

Once we had determined these specific goals, we were able to enter into the planning phase of the method. The decision "what to do" is central. Action for action's sake is never enough; it can lead only to deeper frustration and turmoil. Saul Alinsky's observation is apropos here: "People do not band together in their search for means to alter or modify their circumstances unless they are convinced of the possibility that positive changes can be brought about. . . ." The choice of "what to do" must be made clear and must be seen by everyone as accomplishable. This is best done by continually being aware of the need for *organization, group maintenance,* and *role designation.*

Organization is essential to accomplishing social action's goal. We could not have moved forward without agreement upon regular meeting times and specific tasks for each member of the group. Creating and sustaining the overall organization of the group is an integral part of the action-reflection method. It must be a part of the program from the planning stage to the consummation of the project. Group maintenance and role designation are the essential components of organization.

Group maintenance simply means paying attention to the people involved in the action. Each person has feelings about the group and its purpose. Time must be taken for feedback on group goals and individual feelings. Each of our meetings, for example, was open to a discussion of any person's feelings and thoughts about the entire group's project, even its goals. Each meeting would close with a review of what had just occurred, during which the members would be asked whether anyone had reflections about what he or she had just accomplished or suggestions for the next meeting.

Such a review gives the participants an opportunity to voice their thoughts about the goals of the group and about their own involvement in the meeting. Consensus is always necessary before moving forward. In a vote there are winners and losers, and many times a vote merely determines how the losers will try to affect policy from their minority stance. Group action follows on consensus because all have agreed to act. To reach a consensus takes time, but the time is well spent.

In one of the meetings to assist the parolee, this review was of tremendous value. As we began to discuss why we were involved with the parolee, some group members discovered that they had little interest in him, others found that they were defending him without regard to the reality of his case, and still others found that they had identified themselves with the parole officer and were defending the parole officer in both the discussions and policy decisions. This one meeting alone helped the group move forward with more dispatch and less tension. Some people withdrew from the group when they discovered that they had no genuine interest in what we were doing, while others were able to approach the entire involvement with a clearer understanding of their motivation.

Role designation, or the recognition of gifts and levels of commitment, is the next necessary aspect of organizing social action. Every group has to learn how to divide responsibility among its members, how to ascertain clearly what each is to achieve, how to be sure that each member feels competent and willing to achieve it, and how to hold each one accountable for completion of his or her assignment. If there is to be concerted action, then all of the aspects of role designation must be taken into account. For instance, when some in the group realized they were there for companionship rather than for helping the parolee, they resigned. This recognition of role designation helped the group. The same recognition took place when some who were good at budget management assumed the role of helping the parolee manage his budget.

To expect total commitment from everyone is a recipe for failure in social action. Commitment grows through experience. When one succeeds at something, commitment is not far behind. So as our group began to organize half-way houses for parolees, each victory produced commitment to the total goal of establishing such houses.

3. *Action.* Once a group has determined its goal, it must never act alone. A church group in particular can neither initiate nor sustain effective social action alone. It needs others, and all need to collaborate. There should be constant engagement, cultivation, and maintenance of the following groups: the church authorities, the community change-agents, the consultants, and the supportive persons within the community.

The authorities' explicit or tacit recognition is necessary as long as the group is explicitly religious. But even if it is not overtly a church group, the recognition of its existence by church authorities is a great help in carrying out its task. In the parole group, for example, the fact that a Roman Catholic priest was a member of the sponsoring group was legitimation enough for both the parole officer and the state. It facilitated the prisoner's release.

Such official recognition may sometimes also provide—or make it easier to obtain—such mundane yet so necessary things as money, manpower, and facilities.

One must also collaborate with the community change-agents, the people working inside or outside the established system for changes within the structure. Every social problem has an associated cluster of change-agents, usually people who have been harmed by the inequalities of the system or people who simply see the oppressive situation and want to change it. Each has a different reason for advocating change. Yet the interests of one group may frequently concern another. Collaboration among these groups is essential for effective change and broad-based support. Collaboration is necessary for leadership, perspective, workers, and linkage in action. The task of our group was to collaborate with all those desiring to change the way a person was paroled and to focus this desire toward a realizable goal.

Consultants are another part of the process that gives an added perspective to the task. A consultant is an individual or group who can assist with information, publicity, and judgment in reaching the goal. It is important to secure a network of consultants so that everyone will be as well informed and advised as possible. The purpose of consultation is to expose plans and actions to trusted analysts of similar problems in order to learn from their expertise and experience. A number of consultants were essential to the success of the parole group's action. First to be considered were those associated with the parolee: The parole officer was informative and helpful; a man in the Labor Department for the United States Government suggested the types of jobs that were available to this particular parolee. Then, considering our ultimate aim, we contacted political officials who encouraged the establishment of a half-way house. We also contacted two Methodist ministers who were running a house themselves. These consultants were able to indicate realistically the difficulties of continuing with the program.

Supportive persons are those who are present when the group itself, or individuals within the group, run into obstacles or possible failure. There will always be opposition in social action: Who wants a house with ex-cons next door? Social action deals with structure-change. It deals with power. As a result, those involved in it need as much support as possible from their wives, husbands, professional colleagues, and other kindred spirits in the community. The support of these people will be demonstrated when they commiserate with us, celebrate with us, and constructively criticize us. This demonstrated support is essential to the continuance of any action, since a person must feel that what he or she is doing is worth the time and effort.

4. *Review.* In this last step, each person comes to grips with his

or her own feelings and beliefs about the situation. A review of the basic strategy is necessary, as I mentioned above; but even more important are the persons' analysis of the problem and their feelings toward the action taken.

The theological analysis is discovered in an understanding of Scripture: What is the basic gospel value involved in this specific social action? This gospel value is discovered in an understanding of the Christian stance vis-à-vis social evil. It is discovered in praying that we may act in the Spirit with God's love for all even as we use a form of power to effect the desired results. All three phases are necessary in the theological stance: Scripture, community spirit, and prayer. True reflection in social action involves theology, self, and group planning. These are part of the ongoing program of action-reflection.

Our group had no difficulty in determining the gospel value involved in helping the prisoner. We did uncover problems when we began to see the whole structure as oppressive and began to think about rebuilding it. We had become so accustomed to reading the Scriptures from an individualistic perspective that we had forgotten that salvation occurs in community, that the "world" is a community of evil, and that this evil "world" can exist within a church.

Prayer and worship are part of the Christian life and should never be omitted from the action-reflection method. The use of prayer in a review session must not, however, be a method of running away from a problem; it must be a true reflection upon the situation. Because prayer is sometimes seen as a way to avoid social action, some people are afraid to pray in the midst of social action. Such fears must be faced and overcome. As a group grows in sharing its difficulties in reaching social goals, spontaneous prayer grows, but people should never be forced to pray spontaneously. Prayer can be a beautiful way for the group to express the "why" of its mission and the "who" in whose name they are sent. Moreover, in such small groups any prayer celebration will usually be quite informal, and everyone should be involved in planning the celebration.

Explicit theological reflection has an essential role in the action-reflection method since in social action situations, the religious dimension many times controls the action. Two common examples of how it controls the action are found when religion is mistakenly understood to abhor conflict and when an individual's poverty is presumed to be his or her own fault or

God's will. As to the first, it is true that the use of power always causes conflict and polarization. As a result, someone who has been educated to fear conflict and polarization, as opposed to the gospel message of love, will shy away from using them. Such fear is real and is based on one's religious education. A consultant should be provided to help people deal with such fear. As to the second, seeing poverty as God's will, the Calvinistic work ethic and the image of God as the one who inflicts pain and poverty as a punishment for our sins must be exposed as false. Clearing up such problems enables the group to face the evils present in societal structures with decisiveness and religious conviction.

Action-reflection offers one way to face the unique suffering present in society by joining with those who are convinced that such suffering must be diminished. Hand in hand, we are able to share our anguish in attempting to bring about better societal structures. As we do so we realize that the new structure may easily have sources of injustice hidden in it, too. But if it is more just than the old structures, we have reduced the suffering of some while we look forward to reducing the suffering of more.

The Self and Social Structures

We will suffer. Others will suffer. Each of us is both sufferer and cause of suffering. Admitting these facts and our inability to remain neutral toward suffering imposes on us, as individuals, the duty to do something about suffering. Some ways of dealing with suffering in society were described earlier. Here we intend to reflect upon those norms that assist us in judging our individual, voluntary actions that may lead to deeper suffering. What are some ways of knowing that what we as individuals are doing is life-giving and not destructive of life? The series of questions and principles listed below will help to answer that question.

1. The first question is: Does our individual suffering form, or deform, community? That is, when we accept that suffering (either for ourselves or for others) results from our efforts to rebuild society, we must ask: Is the suffering productive of community, or does it at least offer hope that it will help form community? What we understand by "community" here is important for understanding the question posed. Community can be formed only insofar as each individual is recognized for his or her unique worth in the struggle to establish justice. Each individual

talent is necessary to achieve justice. Suffering can disrupt, or at least fail to build, community when it isolates persons from one another, destroys individuality, and neglects the universal demand of other sufferers for recognition of their situation. Such suffering resulting from our choice warns us that our action may not be life-giving.

2. Does our suffering for justice improve our ability to live creatively with ambiguity, uncertainty, even chaos? After all, these are part of life, so we must be able to live and work in their midst even though there are no criteria for judging with certainty that we are responding properly to them. Take a test case, then. Suppose that a certain woman is convinced that women are not being treated as men's equals. As a result, she spends time away from her family, becomes angry at sexist language, is verbally abused by people who think she is a subversive, and becomes physically tense because no one seems to respect her. The question is, Does her suffering help her to live creatively in that situation? If so, her suffering is life-giving. But where will she – or any of us – get the strength to live that way? Two of the most important factors are proper motivation and proper support. And as we will see in Part Two, the most powerful force behind motivation and support is often one's religion.

3. Does our choice contribute to our self-actualization? If so, it is a source of life. Self-actualization is a process of becoming more and more what we are, everything that we are capable of becoming. It implies progression through a sequential series of stages toward increasingly higher levels of motives and self-organization. We grow in confidence by making good choices and being responsible for them. If we find, therefore, that in following a certain path of suffering we become narrower in our view of the world, that we become self-centered, sarcastic in our humor, and rigid in action, then it is obvious that the suffering is destroying us and reducing our ability to cope with life.

4. Does the choice that causes our suffering result in a growth of love, that is, self-giving? If so, it will build community. But judging whether it is doing so is difficult because we cannot tell by the immediate reaction of others. There is no such thing as instant community. Community and the love relationship take time to build.

5. Does the choice result in a deeper awareness of the ultimate both in our own life and the life of the world? In Christian terms, does the choice allow us to be more sensitive to the Spirit's

movement in our life? Is it deepening our life in the Father, Son, and Spirit? A traditional way of testing whether it does is that offered by St. Paul when he suggests that the fruits of the Spirit are charity, joy, peace, patience, kindness, goodness, faith, gentleness, and self-control (Galatians 5:22,23). When these qualities become more evident in our life, our involvement in the suffering situation is probably a good one.

6. Does the suffering give promise of reaching its goal? It is easy to get so caught up in the suffering situation that we forget the purpose of the suffering. But suffering is a means toward a goal, not an end in itself. So we must be sensitive as to whether it is achieving what it set out to achieve. Thus the necessity to continually reevaluate. A way of doing this is to ask the following two questions.

7. Is our acceptance of suffering faithful to gospel values and historical realities (for instance, the gospel value of justice for all and the historical realities of the Christian tradition to help the needy)? Once we are involved in any social action, we tend to see it as the center of our life. Any course of action continued for some length of time, whether it be a consciousness-raising activity or a strike, for example, changes the situation to some extent: Things are not the same after a month or a year of any form of social action. The question of gospel values must be asked in this new historical context that includes our active suffering. It may be that the structure we seek to substitute for the one we see as evil is worse than the prior one.

8. Are we willing to abandon our suffering and what causes it? Are we willing to give up the role we have so willingly accepted and so painfully engaged in? Only when we are willing to do this are we sensitive to how the suffering or servant role itself can become a source of power and suffering to others. What we are engaged in may have effected change or may be outdated; it may be wrong. Are we willing to admit this and change? Only if we are is this a principled choice.

Asceticism

In the face of our own or another's suffering we often ask: How much suffering can we sustain? Is there any way to know how we will react to suffering?

To play the prophet of social or personal change for the

purpose of answering these questions is a dangerous and usually a mistaken game. Yet common sense tells us that there are ways of knowing how we will react to suffering. The best indicator of future reaction is past reaction: If we have done it before, we will probably do it again. Have we been able to face suffering in the past? If so, granted that we continue our same life-style, we will probably do so in the future.

The style of life that enables a person to deal with suffering is often referred to as an ascetical life. "Ascetical" is an old word, one filled with many meanings and associations. Asceticism conjures up the picture of monks in hair shirts beating and starving themselves to show their contempt for the world and their love of God. Many times the word subtly hints that suffering is good in itself. Such images suggest that we should not use this word. But to avoid the word with its images and associations is to avoid a reality that dominates much talk of suffering and a history that is of benefit to us. In Part Two of this book we will reflect more deeply on this reality and the God it presupposes. Yet the dictionary definition, "self-denial for an ideal," suggests that the term is valuable today. Asceticism does have a part to play in life. It is the basis for our dealing with suffering now and in the future.

Asceticism recognizes that we live life from a root meaning or value that produces patterns of life built to sustain this meaning. For instance, just as a tree sinks its tap root deep into the soil to live, so we sink our living deep into life itself to have a meaning to hold on to. And as the tree stretches to the sun and rain in the very process of living, so we stretch out in time and space in our process of living. In both the tree and ourselves, this stretching out from the center, our root, follows a pattern.

Suffering always challenges our pattern of growth. The tree must deal with shade from a building, or from another tree, that does not allow part of it to grow correctly; it must deal with children digging at its roots or swinging from its branches. If it cannot adapt to this challenge to its pattern of growth, while keeping its deep root, it dies. Our own and others' suffering challenges our pattern for living. The "root" in a person is his or her religion, which we will see more of in Part Two. The "pattern" is the usual way the religion is lived by its adherents. Asceticism refers to how they live their religion and establish their pattern of living.

In traditional Christian asceticism this means basing our life on a heightened sense of who Jesus is and how he is continually present in his Spirit. The Christian pattern of life that seeks to integrate our basic relationship to things, others, and self is our ascetical life. We know that if we always choose what we like best, we become insensitive and self-centered. We know that a pattern of life that focuses upon our own ease results in suffering for others and for ourselves. Many songs of suffering show how selfishness increases the suffering of the singers. We know that two things are necessary to lead a full life: meaning and way. Asceticism is the way we live our meaning.

Part of every way of life is suffering. There is nothing "sick" in acknowledging the pain of the world, personal failure, and inadequacy. It is "sick" only if it turns into self-hatred or self-rejection. To hate and reject oneself as a sinner is equivalent to trying to deny sin. Asceticism, though, admits that we are selfish, we are sinners. It seeks a pattern of life built on this admission. Each of us must consciously seek the pattern of life that reflects the reality of God and our honest recognition of sin.

If we seek and build, if we are conscious of responsible patterning, we will face suffering. We build when we listen to the child who joyfully comes to tell us of his or her discovery. We build when we put in a full day's work for a full day's pay even when we are tired. We build when we do not cut in ahead of the person going into the parking space we wanted. We build when we give money to those in need. We build when we remain silent with ourselves. We build when we join with others to change the prison system. Building is a constant occupation. Sustaining the building, the pattern we are working at, is just as constant and just as filled with concern as is the act of building. This is the life of asceticism. Self-development cannot be its purpose, but it is a product of the very principle of avoiding selfishness. Personal growth is both a prerequisite for sound asceticism and the fruit of it. Asceticism is the basis for facing suffering. And only in a world of ascetical people will suffering be reduced.

Conclusion

We are the singers of the songs of social suffering. We are the sufferer and the cause of suffering. This is a haunting reality, one that is difficult to live with every moment of our life. Just as a person cannot look at the sun for long without being blinded, or think about the death of a loved one for a prolonged time without being overwhelmed with sadness, so to dwell upon our complicity in the suffering of others easily gives rise to feelings of powerlessness and ineptitude. It is difficult to build just structures and easy to destroy them.

In this chapter we heard the songs of suffering and tried to be sensitive to ways of hearing them. Action-reflection is a good method, but it takes time and affects only a small part of the structure. The songs of security, food, possessions, and pills are still sung. One wonders: Will the poor and war always be with us? Will we always want to be Number One as a nation, city, or family? Can we consistently have the fortitude to say no to the evil-causing structures which surround us? Can we ever face our role in causing suffering? Can we ever bring an end to it all?

It is easy to be pessimistic when looking at communal suffering; it is so overwhelming. But just as we can see one dimension of society as evil, so we can see another aspect as good. We can join with those who are willing to share the common purpose of reducing unjust suffering: a community of sufferers striving to lessen suffering. We cannot hear the songs of communal suffering alone; we must hear them together. This is the only way to avoid cynicism and despair. A community offers support and vision in the midst of communal suffering. Our problem is, Where is such a community that supports us and we it, in a holistic way? Where is there a group in which, ideally at least, we may sing together, work together, think together in freedom of expression and in hope of liberation?

* * *

Questions for Individual Reflection
1. List the communities you are a member of (for example, family, church, prayer group, school, sports team, neighborhood).
   a. Which are most significant to you?
   b. Which do you belong to for what you get from them?
   c. Which do you contribute most to in time, work, thought?
   d. Arrange the first three in order of importance to you.
   e. Are any of these communities of and for suffering?
2. Is there anything you would allow your country or church to do that you would not do yourself (for example, forgive those who offended you, give water to the thirsty, refuge to the homeless)?
3. Have you ever used violence to achieve an end?
4. What suffering situation are you in at the moment? Is it life-giving, or

life-destroying?
5. What is the hardest thing for you to do in loving those closest to you? Can you do it twice this week?

Questions for Group Reflection
1. What are some helpful communities of suffering and for the relief of suffering? Each person should name three and give phone numbers.
2. Have you ever attempted to challenge a structural unit of society? Explain.
3. What do you think is the most effective way to diminish suffering in society?
4. Are people or groups as selfish as this book suggests?
5. May violence ever be used to destroy evil?

Conclusion to Part One

We hear a song and react. We witness suffering and respond. Songs and suffering are part of life: By the turn of the dial both can be experienced on radio or television. We react positively to some songs and some forms of suffering, negatively to others. As the tears roll down our cheeks after watching a sad movie, we know that somehow we shared the suffering we witnessed. As the lump in our throat grows to a shout, we know we have felt the vibrations of a song. Seldom do we take time to analyze the shout or the tears. In Part One we took time to look, to think, to suggest ways to act.

We looked beyond the immediate experience of the singers to seek the understanding and the diminishment of suffering. In this looking we found that suffering is a very complex phenomenon. Its complexity was reflected in our analysis of the songs and their language as well as in the relationships among the physical, emotional, and social dimensions of suffering.

We reflected on the physical dimension and spoke of pain and how we deal with it. We looked especially at the patient-doctor relationship and made suggestions for how to deal with the medical staff. The physical dimension of suffering makes us aware of our healthy body and the need for preventive care. We are responsible for our body in sickness and in health.

The second dimension of suffering was the emotional, especially the feeling of loss. We analyzed loss and ways to assist those grieving. When we suffer serious loss, we may be overwhelmed by it. But if we learn to be sensitive to our feelings about people and things now, we will know what is necessary to face loss in the future. Previous sensitivity and dialogue concerning our emotions enables us to deal with loss, no matter how severe.

Communal suffering was the third dimension: "We hurt," not only "I hurt." We analyzed the obligation of lessening structural suffering and gave suggestions for action. Our analysis showed that institutions must attend to their purpose of serving people. Each of us is a member of a number of communities. As we allow the community or institution to run us, instead of our running it, the problems of communal suffering intensify and consequently demand the radical steps suggested in this book.

The complex task of analyzing the songs of suffering—a process of abstraction—becomes simplified in the painful song of one sufferer. Here is the singer's challenge to us: Analysis is useless without synthesis. *We* suffer, not some *dimension* of us. Each of us is not parts but an organic whole capable of being understood and dealt with as a human being, not only as a body, a mind, a set of emotions, or a set of social conditions. No one does or can do our suffering for us. We suffer. No one can relieve our suffering without our help. We are responsible for ourselves and mutually responsible for one another.

Our analysis of suffering in Part One results in a description of suffering: It is that which the singers do and the songs describe. It results in many suggestions for dealing with the physical, emotional, and social dimensions of suffering. It also results in an understanding of suffering that is summarized in the ten following points.

1. *Suffering is a new way of living.* Whether it is suffering from a stubbed toe or from a body destroyed by bone cancer, suffering changes our life. The amount of change is dependent on many factors, but there is always some change.

2. *Suffering challenges us to a deeper relationship with people, things, and self.* As a consequence of suffering we find ourselves seeking physical means to overcome it, people who will help us deal with it, and assurances that we are still loved, valuable, and recognized as some*one*, a unique person, in the midst of so many unrecognizables. We may not accept this challenge to deepen our relationships, but it is there nonetheless.

3. *Suffering diminishes as these relationships deepen.* A relationship develops when we allow someone or something to be real to us and us to him, her, or it. Thus to have a real relationship with a doctor means that in the final analysis the doctor knows what troubles us and as a consequence of his or her relationship to us can make a proper diagnosis. A relationship to a prosthetic device would occur when it becomes so much a part of us that we treat it as an extension of ourselves. None of our relationships can ever be perfect; that is heaven. However, because suffering is multidimensional, it can be decreased by deepening one relationship while another is breaking. For example, we may be dying of a severe physical illness, yet the love shown by those around us will diminish (though not destroy) the suffering.

4. *Everyone suffers.*

5. *We do not suffer alone.*

6. *Suffering has a cosmic dimension.* We are interdependent. Such interdependence does not stop at the boundaries of life and of inanimate things of earth. Each song of suffering is of cosmic proportions because each of us is linked to others.

7. *We cause suffering in ourselves and others.*

8. *Suffering occurs as our relationships to others, self, and things break or diminish.* As relationships decrease, suffering increases. As suffering increases, chaos begins to prevail over cosmos or harmonious relationships.

9. *Although the diminishment of suffering is within our control, suffering itself and some particular manifestations of it are not.*

10. *We are limited as individuals and as a society.* Suffering will always be with us.

These points of understanding resulted from an analysis of the singers and their songs. Yet analysis must always return to the reality it depends upon: the singers of suffering. The questions at the end of each chapter helped us keep this contact with personal suffering. But there is another way of understanding that is beyond scientific analysis. This is a way of looking at the suffering person in relationship to something or someone beyond limit. Since limit is so much a part of our life, we must see life from a different perspective to understand it and the sufferer. We will discover such a perspective in Part Two.

PART TWO

Singing in a New Key

Introduction to Part Two

Suffering challenges who we are and how we lead our life. To be healthy means that we can function to the best of our abilities in the world as we know it. Suffering breaks our world. Like a tree struck by lightning – splintered, shaken, denuded – our world is broken by suffering, and we will never be the same again. What will become of us is a mystery. Yet although the future is mysterious, we do know it depends to a great extent upon what we think the cause of our suffering is and how we seek to rebuild our broken world. Our religious outlook contains both an understanding of the cause of our suffering and a blueprint for rebuilding.

This religious outlook also affects the *intensity* of our suffering. For the intensity of suffering often depends upon what we consider vital and most valuable in life. When we lose the relationship to part of our body, to our spouse, a friend, a job, our home, or God, the way we feel this loss shows how valuable the relationship was to us. Our world as we knew it disappears to the extent that this relationship does. How we rebuild that world with new relationships will depend on whether we feel we have lost everything or whether we feel our life can continue without that person or thing.

Throughout Part Two the word "religion" may seem ambiguous to the ordinary reader. Usually the word "religion" refers to *our* religion or, more often, to *our* church. At the very least it refers to what in our experience we know is religious. In Part Two, and especially in Chapter Four, the word "religion" will refer to religion in general. The word "religions" will refer to the particular religions, such as Christianity or Hinduism.

Whether we speak of religion in general or in particular, we find that religion deals with what is ultimate in our life. In that sense, our religion is our pivotal reason for living. But as soon as we speak of religion in this light, we know that our pivotal reason for living may not be the reason why someone else lives. We know that "my" religion and "your" religion may easily differ – in much the same way as my suffering may be different from yours.

Talking about scholarly definitions of religion and about the relationship between religion in general and suffering in general makes me hesitate. There are always three levels of experience and speech: the personal (my); the personal, yet other (you); and the abstract, yet necessary for communication (words, language structure, ideas). All three levels must be examined in a book on suffering. But the task is difficult because many who read this book are suffering or have suffered a great deal. Such personal suffering makes one wary of abstract explanations and easy hopes of diminishing suffering because the talk seldom conforms exactly to one's experience. What happens when one suffers is that each person creatively adapts to his or her own situation as a way of dealing with what is at first a shocking and inarticulated experience. After much suffering, one learns to handle one's own difficult situation almost automatically and to comprehend one's own suffering in a very specific manner. But it remains difficult, if not impossible, to express what one has learned or to understand another person's explanation of what he or she has learned.

Every sufferer has had the experience of having his or her condition "explained" by people who have had only superficial experience with suffering. This is like explaining the keyboard to a concert pianist. For example, nothing is more ironic to a person steeped in physical pain than to be told that he or she is "God's pet" or that God has allowed him or her the deep privilege of suffering—even though these utterances may have some truth to them.

Those who have suffered deeply are the most wary of uttering clichés about suffering. Experience with the mystery of suffering takes one beyond the realm of ideas. It produces a silence or at least a reticence to express in words the solace that can be found only in shared suffering.

Part Two is nevertheless filled with "abstract" talk about suffering; that is the nature of the written word. But it is also filled with requests for action and sharing, and the questions at the end of each chapter demand more than talk. They require sharing. These reflections are not mine. They are those of myriads of individuals who have shared their suffering with me in all the songs we heard in Part One. These reflections have meant much to others. I hope they will be more than words, that they will be a true communication, a sharing of self through words. These words may be a means through which many who have suffered will reach out to touch other sufferers.

These reflections are divided into four chapters. First we look at some ways that suffering has been understood and dealt with in the world's religions. Suffering, many times, makes us conscious of what is wrong with us or the world; religion can make us conscious of what is right with the world and what must be done to make it better. The songs of suffering can be sung in many keys; the songs can be understood in many ways. The religious key will be examined in Chapter Four.

Yet no one sings a song in many keys at once, nor does anyone practice many religions at the same time. We, especially we Westerners, admit to following one religion and only one, no matter what that one is. Chapter Five will look at the key of the Spirit, one religious interpretation for understanding suffering. Suffering changes our world, makes us conscious of dimensions of it we may never have seen before. But such consciousness may be for good or evil. Will suffering result in a better life for us and others? Or will it destroy us? The Holy Spirit, the presence of meaning – of cosmos – offers us a choice of cosmos over chaos.

This choice must include the one who suffers with us, the source of song, the maker of keys, Jesus. Chapter Six shows how all attempts to understand suffering still find it present in our world. Jesus accepted this presence of suffering and dealt with it. Our dealing with it is found in our imitating Jesus in his reconciling all things to himself and to one another.

Chapter Seven will show how this reconciliation can come about.

CHAPTER FOUR

The Religious Key:
Ways of Understanding and Dealing with Suffering

"Imagine a trembling mother with her baby in her arms, a circle of invading Turks around her. They've planned a diversion; they pet the baby, laugh to make it laugh. They succeed, the baby laughs. At that moment a Turk points a pistol four inches from the baby's face. The baby laughs with glee, holds out its little hands to the pistol, and he pulls the trigger in the baby's face and blows out its brains. Artistic, wasn't it?"
— *Ivan's discourse to Alyosha in* The Brothers Karamazov

"Did heaven look on and would not take their part?"
— *MacDuff in* Macbeth

"The Noble Truth of the origin of suffering is this: It is this thirst (craving) which produces re-existence and re-becoming, bound up with passionate greed. It finds fresh delight now here and now there, namely, thirst for sense-pleasures; thirst for existence and becoming; and thirst for non-existence (self-annihilation).

"The Noble Truth of the cessation of suffering is this: It is the complete cessation of that very thirst, giving it up, renouncing it, emancipating oneself from it, detaching oneself from it."
— Samyutta-nikaya *lvi. II (trans. Rahula)*

* * *

Why does this person suffer? What can we do about it? Answers to these questions have filled the minds and expended the energies of human beings since the beginning of time. As with a song that can be sung in many keys, there are many ways to sing and understand suffering. Yet out of this multitude of answers there are two consistent approaches. One looks to a single answer and solution to suffering; another looks to a complex and interrelated holistic approach.

Those who accept any one of the songs of Part One as *the* description of the solution to suffering follow the first approach. I follow the second. Suffering as it occurs in the individual and in society must be seen as a whole. To neglect this truth is to neglect the truth that suffering is always present, always a part of life. It is true that a toothache can be cured by certain physical procedures, that types of poverty can be eliminated through social manipulation. But suffering itself, which is always with us, cannot be completely destroyed. Cure the tooth and we face our emotions; reduce our feelings of loss and we still must relate to and deal with our culture. This particular singer and song may disappear, but suffering in some fashion is always present.

We must deal with any song of suffering as the leading edge or manifestation of suffering present in each of us. Thus we deal with the aching tooth by treating its physical manifestations, while we are aware that it may be aching because we did not eat the correct foods, and the correct foods were not available because either we were eating junk food or did not have any food, and we did not have any food or ate junk food because our image of self demanded that we approach eating in this unholistic way. . . . We can go on forever. Any singer and song is a manifestation of a much larger song, more complex, more involved – the song of suffering itself.

Our consciousness of why suffering in particular or suffering in the abstract is real is most manifest in our religion. It is our religion that deals with suffering as it is in its totality, not only in its various dimensions. Our religion deals with all suffering but especially with intense suffering, which will be our concern throughout the chapter.

Religions have always faced suffering as it is: whole and entire. Many modern commentators criticize all religion as demanding present suffering for later happiness. These critics manifest their ignorance of religion as it is both lived and preached. Religions have always sought to understand and lessen suffering. Many contemporary thinkers offer a heaven upon earth, while criticizing the various religions for admitting that suffering always exists on this earth. These contemporary thinkers *promise* an earth without suffering, while the religions act to diminish suffering.

This chapter deals with the religious response to suffering. We will thus have an overview of the many existing interpretations of the songs of suffering before moving on in the next chapter to one Christian interpretation.

Definitions: The Language of Religion

Understanding another person's religion is very difficult. But today this understanding is heightened by the new vocabulary and categories that are used in the discipline of religious studies. Before we examine the way religion deals with suffering, we must reflect on the words and categories we will use.

Words

Just as the language of pain, loss, and communal suffering helped us understand the songs of suffering, so will precision in language dealing with religion help us understand the songs of suffering. We look first at a contemporary way of describing religion in many religious studies programs throughout the world. In these classes the word "religion" is used in an inclusive sense. Every culture in the world is accepted as having a religious dimension. Such an inclusive definition may cause problems because our everyday language indicates one restrictive meaning while the academic definition indicates another, broader one. Thus we might use the word "religion" only in connection with those who believe in God, while the broader definition does not demand such belief. We might accept Taoism as a religion, but the broader definition also enables us to speak of Communism as a religion. We might distinguish between religion and church, or even consider the possibility of many different religions in one church.

Categories

Category formation also adds to our difficulty in understanding individual religions. We are accustomed to speaking, for example, about a Christian perspective, a Jewish perspective, a Buddhist perspective. These categories are usually the formations or constructs of the individual person and are based upon his or her image of that particular religion. What indeed is *the*

Christian perspective regarding suffering? Do I find it out by going to "average" Christians and asking them? Do I go to famous Christian intellectuals? Do I ask for it in prayer? Do I seek it in the Christian Scriptures? Behind every category are presuppositions as to what the content of the category is as well as the norm for judging the validity of its content.

A typical example of category formation and the interpretation that goes with it is my description later in this chapter of a devil figure as the cause of suffering. Many religions have such a figure, and it plays differing roles in each of the religions. But in religions that see the universe in terms of personal forces, this figure plays one role; in those that see the universe as one basic reality, it plays another role. I placed the devil figure in the category descriptive of personal forces in the universe because devil figures are found in more of those religions than in any other. I also claim that some Christians see the devil as a spiteful creature who causes suffering while others see the devil as equal to God and causing suffering to everyone, but especially to those who love God. The vast majority of Christian preachers would repudiate any hint that anything or anyone could be equal to God – that would be heresy. Yet in my eighteen years of teaching I have found that whenever I describe the devil as a being subsidiary to God and then proceed to show how a belief in equality of power with God is unorthodox, some Christians always come up to tell me I am wrong. The devil is as powerful as God, they say; otherwise God would destroy the devil. I have included their comments in the formation of the categories that follow.

Category formation, then, is a problem. I present a certain set of categories in this chapter to aid you in understanding how people view and deal with suffering. We must be sensitive to each singer. We cannot presuppose that all Christians have a conviction that God is responsible for suffering, or that all Buddhists believe that ignorance and desire are the sources of suffering. Practically, it is best to read the views presented here as those of individuals we may possibly meet. For we cannot be sure that because someone belongs to a certain church, he or she holds one particular view.

It is always difficult to understand another's religion. Judaism, Christianity, and Islam have seldom attempted to understand other religions as religion. Instead they defined their own religion as religion; everything else was not religion. Other cultures were heretical or pagan; these people did not have true religion. Thus large masses of people were written off as following mere philosophy, ethical systems, or superstition rather than a religion. This was done because each of these religions believed it had *the* truth.

In attempting to understand the religious dimension of suffering, we face the same difficulty as these religions faced: the necessity of allowing others to maintain their interpretation of suffering and their manner of coping with suffering. Hearing someone else's explanation of suffering, especially in the midst of personal suffering, is a great exercise in personal discipline. Suffering challenges our way of understanding the world, our God, our life. Another explanation of suffering is as challenging to our sanity as suffering itself is, since we must make some sense of suffering. Intense suffering pounds into our life the possibility that our God, our life, our world may be false. Others' explanations challenge our personal religion as those persons manifest themselves to us in the ways they pray, the cards they send, the advice they give, the sincerity they show as they explain suffering to us.

Definitions

The scope of the religious dimensions of suffering is found in the definition of religion itself. From the standpoint of a believer, religion is what gives him or her direction. It is what he or she celebrates, believes, and professes as ultimate. It is what gives his or her life meaning. If we try to give a definition of religion that takes into account all the believers of the world, we can define it as a system of symbols giving unity, meaning, and purpose to human life by being a means of ultimate transformation. (This is a definition of religion dependent upon F. Streng, *Understanding Religious Life* (Belmont, Cal.: Dickenson, 1976) and C. Geertz, "Religion as a Cultural System," in *Anthropological Approaches to the Study of Religion*, M. Banton, ed. (New York: Harper and Row, 1966).) As a system of symbols, the many aspects of religion are interlocked, one depending on the other for its meaning. Shift the meaning of a symbol ever so slightly or emphasize one value over another and the religion changes. For example, the American emphasis on democracy and individual rights produced significant changes in the major American religions. The present organization of the Episcopal Church is a result of the American way of life. The current struggles in

Roman Catholicism over the authority of the bishop and the role of pastoral councils is another.

Religion gives unity, meaning, and purpose to life, makes it a cosmos. Not that we can articulate that meaning; many times people who are religious cannot clearly express how their faith gives them a vision of self and the world. But it does. When we speak of having a vision of life, a world view, we must be sensitive to the fact that this vision many times is not articulated, just as our visions of ourselves are not articulated. Yet even though our vision of ourselves is not articulated, we do act from it. For instance, when we buy clothes or a car or go to a movie, we have a sense of what we like or do not like—what is "us." We have no need of psychoanalysis to discover our identity in order to buy a pair of pants, yet we buy the pants in the light of our vision of who we are. The same is true of our religion: We act out of a sense of what is most important in our life—what is defined in our description of religion as giving unity, meaning, and purpose to life. We may know what our vision is only when we look back at all our choices. So in speaking of our vision of self and world, either in this context or later, we must be aware that even though we may have neither the creativity nor the personal awareness to write or speak about this vision, this does not mean we do not have one.

Our "vision" is what we understand to be both the ultimate transformation and the means to achieve this transformation. The "ultimate transformation" is what we envision as life at its best; that is why it is an ultimate. In our religious life we regularly gather together with those who share our vision, who agree on what the ultimate transformation will be. We also gather regularly with those with whom we sense an agreement upon the means to bring about this transformation. The creeds, the worship, the individual prayer, the ethical demands—all these are means through which the ultimate transformation takes place. The believers, gathered together, proclaim that their vision of the world is the correct one, that ultimately this truth, this worship, this way of treating one's neighbor and the world is *the* way of changing the world for the better.

This vision of the believers as described in our definition of religion must be a unified vision, for without clear vision we are blind. Religion is our pivotal way of seeing the world. Without it we have no center, no clear song. Organized religion, as found in churches, for instance, may, according to our general definition, include many different religions. This is especially true today in the midst of severe cultural changes where the churches are the focus of much religious conflict. But even within each church there is a constant struggle to sustain a vision or way of life common to that particular church. Our religious life always seeks a unified vision of the world and is not satisfied until it is achieved.

Suffering challenges both the religious vision and the religion as a means of ultimate transformation. Suffering as it comes to us and to others makes it evident that we hurt, even in prayer; hate, even in worship; doubt, even in proclaiming the truth. Suffering clearly suggests that beneath the unity, meaning, and coherence of the religious vision is chaos. Now. In this singer, chaos is manifest. This chaos, manifested through suffering, challenges the religious vision and all its promises of means and visions of ultimate transcendence.

While suffering challenges the religious vision, suffering itself suggests a type of vision. When we point out that suffering is the painful consciousness of that within our world which is not what we expect it to be, we see how the religious vision and suffering are intimately connected. Both visions deal with expectation, but from different sides—religion principally looking to what will be and should be, suffering to the lack of what ought to be: My tooth should be whole, my body without this cancer, my life without my hatred of my co-workers. Suffering points beyond itself to a different kind of life: one without suffering, one we would expect if suffering were not present. Suffering calls attention to the limitation and insufficiency of this world; religion describes and offers means of overcoming these deficiencies.

These comments on religion and suffering reflect contemporary concerns and scholarship. Suffering is now being seen from a holistic perspective. Hence an investigation into the why and the how of suffering must consider factors beyond biology. This holistic concern is the thrust of this book. Religion, in its general sense, is also being seen in a holistic manner. In trying to understand religious life we do not reduce it to only one element such as belief or the supernatural. Thus, although the supernatural is a vital dimension to many religions, when we try to understand religion in general we cannot limit ourselves to supernatural explanations for the existence of religion. One does not have to believe, for example, in God to be called religious even though one's particular religion believes in God.

Consequently an investigation into the why and the how of religion looks to the expectations, practices, values, and belief systems of concrete human beings, not solely to revealed truths from a supernatural realm, for an understanding of a particular religion. The result is that religion may be seen to exist among people who would reject the religionist label in particular even while immersed in religious practices in general.

We will examine two categories of religion: the classical and the modern. A religion is placed in one category or the other on the twofold basis of when it began and what beliefs it originally held. The classical forms of religion began before the seventeenth century and believed that this physical world has its basis in another, non-physical one. The modern forms of religion began in the seventeenth century and believed that only the human person, this universe, and what we can experience are real. These categories, together with the definition of religion I used, enable us to understand the hopes and expectations associated with suffering. When our individual religion is challenged by the suffering situation, many visions compete to replace it. Some of these are classical in form. We are accustomed, for example, to recognizing the religious language of Christianity or of Hinduism. But there are modern religions that we may not recognize. They too offer us a vision of life and how it should be transformed. Perhaps this may be better expressed in another way. The cry "Where is God?" that may be heard in a suffering situation is actually a cry for a god who or which will bring this chaos of suffering into a cosmos of living. There are many "gods" ready to answer the call. Let us look at these "gods" or visions of ultimate transformation.

Classical Religion and Why We Suffer

The classical religions are Judaism, Christianity, Islam, Hinduism, Buddhism, Taoism, Confucianism, and Shinto. Each, in its own way, speaks of suffering and offers "correct" ways of responding to it. Suffering, although recognized by all religions, is a different problem to each, since each religion is a different system of symbols. The differences among these systems will be seen in the brief and necessarily somewhat superficial descriptions in the following paragraphs.

In speaking about the classical forms of religion we must make an immediate distinction between those religions that see the world as resulting from personal forces and those that do not. The first group may ask, "Why does God do this to us?" This question reflects their belief in a divine power or transcendent being with personal attributes. Their explanation of suffering follows from their view of the relationship between creature and creator. The second group, however, conceives of the ultimate in impersonal terms. To them, the world and humans are eternal, uncreated, and one. To these religions, suffering is accepted and dealt with as a part of life, not as a challenge to it.

With this basic division in mind, let us look at some typical responses to suffering by those classical forms of religion that see the world as formed by personal forces. Those religions see God as eternal, all-powerful, all-knowing, and personal. This way of understanding God has given rise to three basic models or ways of understanding why God causes or allows suffering to exist: the instrumental, the punitive, and the redemptive. We can see these models still used not only in these classical religions but in contemporary life outside of these religions.

The *instrumental* model of suffering is found, for instance, in the Islamic belief that suffering is an instrument in the purposes of God; in Christianity, that God made Jesus perfect through suffering (Hebrews 12:3-10); in Marxism, that suffering is an inherent part of bringing about the revolution. In any discussion of suffering this way of understanding the "why" of suffering comes to the fore as we tell one another that few good things are produced without pain or as we ask how we can develop into mature persons without suffering. The belief is that suffering is an instrument, sometimes sharp, sometimes blunt, of individual and communal development. A personal God uses it to bring about his goal for humanity.

Suffering considered as *punishment* changes the emphasis slightly yet significantly. Punishment highlights the judgmental character of a personal God. We suffer because we or others have sinned. Suffering is a way of righting the imbalance of evil over good. As Rabbi Ruba (1500 C.E.) said, "If a man sees that painful suffering visits him, let him examine his conduct." This approach is found in many prayer books of classic religionists. But classic religion is not alone in such an approach: The blood of many people flows in reparation for the sins of their colonial forefathers; a woman in public office is hounded from it for an offense committed in her teens; those who commit crimes against society are punished for past deeds. The model of suffering as a punishment for wrongdoing is evident to anyone who makes a child suffer because of some misdeed. It is a short step to complete the circle and ask of the sufferer what he or she has done wrong, because suffering is supposedly always linked to wrongdoing. As a Sufi saying has it, "When you suffer pain, your conscience is awakened, you are stricken with remorse and pray God to forgive your trespasses."

The belief in suffering as *redemptive* is found in many stories and songs: Someone takes upon himself or herself the sins and burdens of others so that all will be free of the consequences of sin. In this view, whenever anyone suffers so that others may live, redemption occurs. The prophets of Israel make this clear in describing the role of the Babylonian captivity in the nation's life. Isaiah summarized it when he said, "By his suffering shall my servant justify many, taking their faults on himself" (Isaiah 53:11). John's Gospel applies this same principle to Christianity when John the Baptist claims that Jesus is the one who takes away the sins of the world (John 1:29).

These are three common ways of understanding why we suffer. Anyone reading this book probably uses one or more of these to understand suffering as it occurs in his or her life. The phrase "God's will" usually refers to a God who knows all and is Lord of all; thus our suffering fits in some way into God's way of doing things either instrumentally, punitively, or redemptively. Notice that in each of these ways God is very much involved in our suffering. God is responsible for it as its direct cause or as allowing it to happen. Notice too that all three of these ways of understanding suffering are also part of our daily experience of suffering and of dealing with those we consider as immature or less knowledgeable than ourselves.

Some religions have personified the cause of suffering not in a good God but in a powerful devil god, angel, or other kind of superior being. The personification of the evil principle in a devil figure is, at the same time, a reflection of the religion's concept of the divine. We see, for instance, a gradual evolution in Judaism and Christianity of the idea of devil as well as of the idea of God. It parallels the challenge to Judaism and Christianity made by Zoroastrianism and Manichaeism. Both of these religions demonstrated a hatred of all material things. The body and all created matter were seen as evil. The devil figure who was seen as the lord of material things became, with time, almost equal to God, who was the lord of the spiritual kingdom. The dualism of Christianity and Judaism represented by the idea of creature and creator became exaggerated in these religions so that there were two gods: one evil, one good. Christianity, in arguing against this idea, nevertheless took on an emphasis that is still prevalent among some Christians. It portrayed the devil as responsible for evil and suffering.

The personification of evil is also found among some Hindu sects. In the Vedas, a collection of sacred documents, the god Yama, the Lord of Death, is both frightening and handsome in appearance. Suffering, in the Vedas, is basically a part of the universe of being; it needs to be seen in the perspective of this world as a whole. The personification of the cause of suffering in an evil god is such that we are ultimately driven beyond all personification to the realization that all things are one and that suffering itself is impermanent and thus an illusion. Hinduism accepts growth in truth as a fact of life. Thus at a certain stage of life one can accept the source of evil to be a god, only to realize, when such belief is taken seriously, that such an acceptance is impossible. Taking the one conviction seriously should drive us, according to this religion, to realize the impermanence and illusory nature of all things.

Some religions focus on the "self" as a cause of suffering. The "self" is seen as a cause of evil and of suffering among Christians who believe in original sin. Whether it was caused by the selves of Adam and Eve or of a contemporary human, oneself or another "self," suffering is seen to occur when the self opposes the will of God. In this view, the present state of humanity's alienation and the suffering resulting from it is caused by the selfish self. We suffer, therefore, because other selves (persons) cause us to suffer by being selfish, or we cause ourselves to suffer by being selfish.

This idea of a selfish self can be seen from a different perspective in the Hindu belief in Karma. The Hindus believe that the acts done in our former lives never leave us. The individual selves remain bound to the world and reappear in future existences, still attached in diverse ways to those actions. This attachment, of course, is the cause of our present suffering. Thus the self that does not do the duties appropriate to its state in life or does not reduce its desires, sets itself up for lifetimes of suffering because it does not detach itself from the impermanent. The self, not realizing what truth is, causes its own suffering. The truth, in this view, is that only that which is permanent is real. Any attempt to retain our individuality binds us to what changes. We must awaken to the truth that lies beyond selfishness, and we will know this truth when we are no longer selfish.

To sum up: When "Why do we suffer?" means "Who makes us

suffer?" these religions explain the cause as God, some devil figure, or the self.

However, not all classical religions trace evil or good to a personal cause. Some suggest other ways to understand the existence of suffering. "Why are we suffering?" we might ask. Taoism and Confucianism suggest that we are suffering because we are out of harmony with the Way (Tao) or the Cosmic Order. If we were in harmony, we would not suffer. Some modern religions say something similar to this when they suggest that we suffer because we are not acting according to our nature.

Some early Greek religions have a simple, straightforward answer to why we suffer: "It's fate. That's the way it is," they say. And in saying this they imply that suffering is part of the way the universe is constructed. Actually if we look at the instrumental, punitive, and redemptive models we can see how they can be understood from such a perspective by replacing the word "God" with the word "nature." Thus we suffer because suffering is a law of nature. Such natural suffering, if accepted, is how we grow to be a better person (instrumental); or suffering comes because we break a law of nature by, for instance, not getting enough exercise (punitive); or suffering is nature's way of developing the human race by having one person suffer to develop something worthwhile (redemptive). It's a law of nature, they suggest, that nothing worthwhile happens unless our suffering makes it happen.

"Why do we suffer?" Some religionists answer that we suffer because something or someone prevents us from being what we should be. These religions (Christian Science, for example) admit that suffering is occurring, but they tend to see the cause of the suffering as a negative reality—e.g., negative thoughts rather than positive ones. Such views of suffering are usually based on the conviction that any evil is a privation or absence of being or goodness.

Some interpreters of Christianity follow the general thrust of this negative approach to evil in trying to avoid holding God responsible for it. They suggest that God can create only the good, that he is responsible for all that exists. But evil may arise when, for some reason, the goodness of things, their being, cannot be complete. Anything that is contingent can not-be. Whenever we freely limit the goodness of things, we cause evil. Suffering follows as a consequence of the evil we cause. Our first defection from God and the consequent vitiation of our nature was the Fall. We suffer as a result of that voluntary fall from the source of goodness and life.

Many Hindus and Buddhists, of course, hold that suffering is passing and therefore is of no real consequence, since the only reality is that which is one and permanent. Things that change are not permanent and thus are not real. Suffering is something that changes and thus is not real. It does not exist for one who can perceive reality as it is. We find a tendency toward this same type of argument among some modern religions. For instance, they say that when we attain psychological maturity we should be able to cope with suffering because when society has advanced in mature social relationships, suffering will disappear.

Nowadays there are a variety of answers to the question of why we suffer, and all the answers are in terms of what we understand the ultimate to be: God, impersonal forces, nothingness, a manifestation of reality, or humanity. Each religion has to find a way to fit suffering into its view of what constitutes the unity, meaning, and purpose of the world. One cannot talk about a religious view of suffering without talking about a religion's entire symbol system.

We have found five basic answers to the question of suffering: We suffer because God causes suffering; because someone or something else causes it; because we ourselves cause it; because the world is constituted with suffering as part of it; and finally the answer that the question itself makes no sense because it is based on the false presupposition that our changing world is real, when actually all suffering and change do not participate in the permanence of reality itself. Interestingly enough, not one of these answers to the why of suffering ever carries over into a passive approach to the suffering individual. All the classical forms of religion suggest that believers should actively engage in reducing suffering among their fellow sufferers.

Classical Religion and Coping With Suffering

The classical forms of religion teach us how to cope with human suffering by stressing what may be called "right prayer" and "right living." Here again there is no one way peculiar to each religion; we find these various ways shared by all of them, although the reasons for using them differ in each religion.

Prayer refers here to both individual and ritualistic prayer. It is expressed in ritual action, consecration, and mystical union.

Ritual action copes with suffering in many ways: for example, by enlisting the support of the religious community as in Jewish mourning practices of Shiva or the Catholic Mass; or by placing sufferers in a positive frame of mind by putting them in contact with their ultimate concern and consequently relativizing the suffering. Some ritual actions are believed to reduce suffering itself, as in forms of faith healing.

Consecration is prayer and life-style committed to a significant religious figure—for example, Krishna or Jesus. Prayer is a communication with this most significant figure in the religion. Our suffering takes on a meaning because of our relationship to this significant religious figure. At the same time our consecration to him or her opens up patterns of endurance, compassion, and forgiveness because we want to base our life upon the object of our consecration, who has also suffered.

Mystical union is consecration brought to completion by accomplishing oneness with the ultimate in our life. We see this in the Eastern religions, where the ultimate identity of each of us is found in the permanent (Brahman); or in the far East, in Tao, where we can reach an inner perception of and unity with Tao. The union is with that which is beyond the here and now. In this union there is no suffering.

Right living looks toward the diminution of suffering by erasing its immediate cause. It sets the stage for a world free of the suffering caused by humans. Judaism, for instance, has given us many principles of justice and concern that are found in the Scriptures. The statement of God in Hosea 6:6, " . . . what I want is love, not sacrifice," sets the prophetic theme of justice and love for all. And Nathan's statement to David, "You are the man" (2 Samuel 12:7), i.e., you are responsible and accountable to God for the suffering you cause, places the burden upon the individual to relieve suffering. The Christian's obligation vis-à-vis suffering is found both in the Sermon on the Mount (Matthew 5:1-12 and Luke 6:20-26) and the example of Jesus, who went about "doing good" in healing the blind, the lame, and the deaf. Islam's *Five Pillars* includes a direct attack on poverty and demands the giving of alms. As the Quran says, "Did he not find you wandering and give you guidance? As for the orphan, then, do him no harm; as for the beggar, turn him not away" (*Smriti* xciii). For the Hindu, right living consists in specifying duties for each stage of life. If lived, they decrease the suffering in the world. In essence, one should cause harm to no one. Buddhism and Hinduism find a common bond in a compassion that seeks unity with the suffering of others in order to destroy all suffering.

Right living is the goal of every religion. But obviously it has not been attained, and we remain in our suffering. Yet it cannot be emphasized enough that every classical religion has the diminution of suffering as an essential part of its world view (unity, meaning, and purpose) and as one of its means of ultimate transformation. One can only imagine, as the classical forms of religion continue to diminish in our Western world, what we will be like in the future without these religious impulses to deal with the suffering in society and in individual life.

Modern Religion:
The Why and How of Suffering

Contemporary Western society is moving away from the classical forms of religion. Yet, since all humans are religious in some way, new forms of religion have come to take the place of the old.

Without going into the various "civil religions," Nationalisms, and Marxisms, we will use the work of F. Streng, *Ways of Being Religious* (New York: Prentice-Hall, 1977), to describe these modern religions' ways of coping with suffering. Of Streng's eight ways of being religious, we will focus on two: achieving an integrated self through creative interaction, and the new life through technocracy.

What differentiates the classical from the modern religions is that what is *part* of the way of transformation in the classical forms—for example, care of the body, work—becomes the ultimate in these modern forms. A number of religions, for instance, foresee a time when we will live forever with new bodies at the end of this world, while justice will reign along with understanding, trust, and love. But all such religions relate these characteristics of a new world to God. Modern religions do not. They look toward an ultimate transformation, described below, and say that humans of themselves can and must achieve this transformation. This is why sometimes these forms of religion are described as humanistic.

Suffering, in the first modern way of being religious, resides principally in the "psychological" dimension of the individual. We wall ourselves into a room of loneliness and alienation because we lack love, personal integrity, relatedness to others. This is why suffering occurs. If we develop those positive characteristics we now lack, we will be whole and without suffering. We can develop if we experience empathic responses, grow in self-acceptance, and respond to others. Of course we cannot do it alone; mental health movements and social education are necessary to lessen suffering. This way of being religious does not promise to do away with suffering all at once; no religion does. But it is convinced that if the "sins" of loneliness can be replaced by the virtues of love, there will come about an ultimate transformation, and suffering will cease.

Another way sees the source of suffering in our lack of control over our environment. Because we lack this control, we die. If we used and developed the proper technologies, we could have physical comfort and personal security. The reason we are sick or we suffer is that we have not spent the money and time to seek the causes and controls of the agents of suffering. We can find these causes if we find the laws of nature that control the world. Using our minds, not our emotions, we can design a utopia. We must choose between rational design and death in a world quickly coming to the point of total suffering and self-destruction.

These two modern ways of being religious, then, speak of the causes of suffering: our mind and our way of dealing with nature. They also offer ways to reduce suffering: love and rational control. Yet these religious approaches to suffering, so often proclaimed in media and literature, have not removed suffering or persuaded us all to agree on *the* cause of suffering. These forms, like the classical ones, still need to be tried consistently and by large numbers of people before we can see if they can diminish suffering.

Conclusion

Each religion offers a description, diagnosis, and prescription for suffering. Each human lives by some kind of religion. Those of us involved in a community of suffering or a community to relieve suffering realize that the religious dimension of others is that which is most vital to them. In dealing with the suffering of others, their religion—that which gives unity, meaning, and purpose to their life—plays a crucial role in their way of handling suffering. If our religion disintegrates in the midst of suffering, the suffering is intensified; if our religion sustains us, the suffering is lessened. The holistic nature of suffering allows us to describe the physical, social, and psychological characteristics of suffering. But what gives suffering its meaning and value is the person's religion.

We have looked at some of the religions that people live by. We have seen what they have to offer by way of explaining and dealing with suffering. In the next chapter we will look at one religion, Christianity, and one theology within Christianity to try to understand the how and the why of suffering.

* * *

Questions for Individual Reflection
1. Do you think your religion is helpful to you when you suffer?
2. Have you ever suffered so deeply that you gave up your religion—even if only for a moment?
3. What are three aspects of your religion that you like? Dislike?
4. Of the three models of why we suffer, which makes the most sense to you?
5. Does prayer have a place in your suffering?

Questions for Group Reflection
1. Have you known anyone who ceased practicing his or her religion as a result of suffering (e.g., the claim of many feminists that their church is sexist)?
2. Who has most to do with why we suffer? God? Devil? Self?
3. Which of the three quotations at the start of this chapter is the most challenging to your understanding of suffering?
4. What can the group do regarding suffering in general?
5. What can the group do to relieve the suffering of those who sing the songs of emotion?

CHAPTER FIVE

A Song of Our Own: A New Consciousness, A Holy Spirit

" . . . *he broke the bread, and offered it to them. Then their eyes were opened, and they recognized him; and he vanished from their sight.*"

—Luke 24:30-31, NEB

" . . . *My God, my God, why hast thou forsaken me?*"

—Matthew 27:46, NEB

"Death is swallowed up; victory is won! O Death, where is your victory? O Death, where is your sting?"

—1 Corinthians 15:54, NEB

* * *

We are alive when we have our own song. We find ourselves humming the song, hearing it, feeling its vibrations. We are one with it. It is ours, yet it is more than ourselves because others, in their way, may share the same song. When we have our own song it becomes part of us, for a song is not a song unless it is sung, played, heard, and enlivens both singer and hearer. I cannot help remembering three instances that demonstrate clearly what it means to have a song of our own.

The first was when our eldest son began to sing. He knew we enjoyed his attempts at song. Whenever we were in the living room, he would balance himself on a small, round footstool and sing *his* song. We would listen and encourage him. As he sang and we reacted, the sound got louder, his body swayed, his hands moved. All of us were part of his song. We were present to each other in and through the song.

There were times when he would get up to sing on the footstool when no one was there. But he would soon climb down and go about his play—no use singing if no one was there to hear.

Another instance was when a young folksinger in California returned home after her first success: "They loved it! They sang! Fantastic!" Words stumbled from her lips, trying to find the correct posture in front of this new reality. Her song lived. The difference between a successful concert and a mere recital is the consciousness of a mutual presence of audience, musicians, and music.

The third instance was a hot afternoon in Milwaukee. The large, dusty field was filled with people of all ages. We had come to hear a famous contemporary orchestra. As the day progressed, the audience laughed, clapped, felt the music in every part of their being. The music became part of everyone; we could hardly distinguish between the music and ourselves.

When a song becomes part of us it becomes a true expression of our self. It symbolizes us. Thus we need more than words and instruments, the physical part; we also need a context that is the complex relationship between singer, song, and hearer. When everything is right a song enlivens us. It cannot exist without us, yet it is more than we. It gives us a new view of life, yet we are still ourselves. It enables us to be present to something that is more than ourselves. We become part of this "more" in a concert, in humming the song during the day, walking in step with others singing the same tune. A song gives us a center. It places us in harmony with something and someone beyond ourselves—a spiritual presence that is more than hearer and listener.

This presence is enlivening, spontaneous, attractive, joyful. There may be times when we fear it is too intoxicating—for instance, when we feel ourselves caught up in the military marches of the United States, Russia, or France, or in the fanaticism of a football or baseball cheer, a deep religious chant, or a rock concert. Once we feel the intoxication, however, we usually accept it because we know this is a good presence we are in (patriotism, play, religious devotion). The song envelops us in this presence, which becomes a part of us. We like it; we want to keep the feelings associated with it. These feelings are emotions pointing to cosmos: a unified, meaningful, purposeful life.

The song of suffering is a similar, yet different, experience. As we concluded in Part One, suffering changes our life. As suffering intensifies, a new presence, pain, combined with the feelings associated with loss, takes hold of us. As people react to our pain and suffering we may feel a closeness to them or a distance from them. Their nod, their frown, their expression of friendship help compose our song. In feeling the loss implicit in suffering we become conscious of new presences as well as of absence. In intense suffering there may even come a point when the feeling of absence overcomes that of presence. It may be the absence of our health, of our spouse, of our friend, or of a just community. We feel what might be described as chaos: an absence of unity, meaning, and purpose in our world. When we were healthy, married, friends, or part of a just community, we sang the song of joy. In suffering we lose that song. Our world, as we know it, has left us. As a result of the suffering we feel the loss of the presence that makes life worthwhile. We have lost our song. Chaos is present.

Suffering exists to the extent that chaos reigns because we either do not understand the suffering or because we cannot control its causes. As a result of this lack of understanding and control, our relationships to things, people, and life's meanings break down. This, as we concluded in Part One, results in suffering and is experienced as chaos.

The chaos present in the life of a terminally ill patient and the chaos present in Miss America's sobs at the end of a transient reign are quite different. Yet we all know that no matter how much chaos is present in a situation, the way we deal with that situation makes the crucial difference. In other words, our consciousness of what the suffering is all about is of supreme importance for what we experience and how we deal with it.

If, for example, I have an illness and I think it is terminal, I am conscious of this illness in a different way than if I think it is the flu. So too if I think that the women complaining about male oppression are frustrated old maids, I look at their complaints differently than if I see them as demonstrating societal injustice. Consciousness of why I am suffering makes a lot of difference in how much I suffer. Many things are the same as they were before: the people, my past experiences, my abilities. Yet what I experience is quite different. Perhaps an illustration will clarify my point.

Let us imagine this scene: Pictures lie scattered over the floor – pictures of the dead body of a small girl, of sheet music, of a guitar, a pair of glasses, three adults dancing in a circle, a poem written on fine stationery, and a blind person frantically feeling for the doorknob. These pictures mean nothing unless we know the story behind them. Individually they are intriguing and complete, but only when put together do they tell a story. As we become aware of how they can fit together, we can pick up the pictures in different sequences. Inspired by various moods, we can arrange them to tell a different story each time. Let us suppose, though, that there is one story, one consciousness, that obviously makes more sense than the others: one that holds our interest while being faithful to each of the pictures and that leaves us convinced that it is the best way to tell the story. Yet there are always many stories present in the pictures. Just as there was one Vietnam War, so there are many stories about it. But somehow the writer put all the parts together in the most meaningful fashion for himself or herself and for others so that the writer can claim this as the true story.

Suffering and songs are much like stories: They are composed of bits and pieces, but we experience them whole and entire. The nature of this experience depends in part on the context or mood we are in; and this mood, in turn, results in different interpretations, feelings, and reactions.

The process of uncovering a hidden structure, meaning, and way of seeing is called consciousness-raising. It is a process in which we become "conscious" of what is always present.

Consciousness-raising occurs, for example, when we are able to see these pictures in a new way. Or suppose that we go to a junkyard, get all the parts needed for a car, bring them home, and build a car. When we learn how to put the parts together, our consciousness about what a car is has been raised. Or again, suppose we look at a picture that has three lions in it, but at first all we see is trees. When we finally see the shape of one of the lions, we can soon see all of them. The lions were there in the drawing all the time, but it is only when we become conscious of their shape that we actually see them. The "facts" are the same before and after our discovery, but what we see is quite different when we have a new consciousness.

Obviously there are an infinite number of "consciousnesses," ways of understanding life. There are also an infinite number of ways of understanding suffering. The last chapter showed some of these understandings. This chapter will reflect on one of these consciousnesses that bring unity, meaning, and purpose to our life—the Christian one.

When we suffer or share the suffering of others, we are conscious of a presence in their song. Is it the presence of cosmos, or of chaos? We change as a consequence of our own suffering and the suffering of others. This change occurs as we become conscious of the cosmos or chaos in the suffering. Whether and how intensely we accept the suffering situation as chaos or cosmos; whether the chaos present in the suffering becomes so intense that we lose our will to live; and whether the cosmos present in the suffering becomes evident so that we live more intensely—all these possibilities depend on our consciousness of whether this presence enables us to see our life as more unified, purposeful, meaningful.

In what follows I will describe a type of consciousness that may be present to you. I believe it is inherent in every suffering situation. This belief is part of my faith-stance and naturally influences my understanding of suffering. I believe that there is a God and that this God sustains all things. As a consequence, God is present even in suffering. The description of God's presence that I give here is in general terms. Because it is in general terms, it will not fit the details of every situation and may at times seem exaggerated. But did you ever notice that what might be exaggerated in one situation might not be in another? A description of the joy of walking up one step may be exaggerated and boring to one who can walk, but to the one-year-old, climbing a step is the joy of a lifetime; to one unable to place one foot in front of another because of multiple sclerosis, the grace and ease of a teenager running up the stairs is a source of overwhelming envy and amazement. The consciousness I describe here is a gift. It comes to some, not to others. The intensity with which we experience it is also a gift of circumstances, birth, environment. It is a consciousness of a holy presence, of a God who is with us always, even in the depths of suffering. The hidden structure of the reality of suffering is that God is present in what at first seems chaos or even death.

The New Song: A Holy Presence

Chaos. Nothing works, people do not get along, ideals are not given life, our body is racked by pain. Over chaos "in the beginning" the Spirit of God hovered (Genesis 1:2), and the earth took form; over chaos a strong driving wind came and filled the Apostles with a new life that united the devout Jews who had gathered in Jerusalem that first Pentecost (Acts 2). Over the chaos of physical suffering, emotional anguish, and social abuse, a visionary proclaimed that he saw:

. . . a new heaven and a new earth; the first heaven and the first earth had disappeared now, and there was no longer any sea. I saw the holy city, and the new Jerusalem, coming down from God out of heaven, as beautiful as a bride all dressed for her husband. Then I heard a loud voice call from the throne, "You see this city? Here God lives among men. He will make his home among them; they shall be his people, and he will be their God; his name is God-with-them. He will wipe away all tears from their eyes; there will be no more death, and no more mourning or sadness. The world of the past has gone."

Then the One sitting on the throne spoke: "Now I am making the whole of creation new," he said. "Write this: that what I am saying is sure and will come true." And then he said, "It is already done. I am the Alpha and the Omega, the Beginning and the End." (Revelation 21:1-6)

A new song is present.

The songs of suffering and our analysis of them show that each of us in our suffering has a pivotal way of coping with suffering, a center from which we deal with it. Christianity identifies *the* center (the context, the presence) as the Spirit of God. We cope best with suffering by being conscious of God's presence in the suffering situation. All the other ways of coping with suffering become new in this context. Without this awareness all the other ways of coping with suffering are stopgap measures that only help us face suffering momentarily.

This Spirit is the unique personal perspective (historical background, horizon) against which everything else is seen. From this perspective we see that within the chaos, fear, and guilt of suffering is also the reality of God's love bringing cosmos out of chaos. The scriptural passages just referred to indicate this. The new consciousness of this presence offers us a choice of living differently, of living with a new Spirit.

This Spirit is not restricted or restrictive. It goes where it wills. It is free. The Spirit-life has about it a spontaneity that seems chaotic to those without this vision: People speak about absent realities, walk to a martyr's death, prophesy against established values and visions. Indeed, to many who have never tasted this cup, those who sing the new song seem drunk (see Acts 2:12-15). They simply do not see things the way the rest of the world sees them. Those who sing in this way are not in a different world, but they see the world in a different way. They see in the world around them realities they and others have never seen before. Their consciousness has been raised, has become something new.

This Spirit at the same time reconciles us with these new realities. It unites us with the center of all reality, which we call God. God is the center of the song the universe sings.

And for anyone who is in Christ, there is a new creation; the old creation has gone, and now the new one is here. It is all God's work. It was God who reconciled us to himself through Christ and gave us the work of handing on this reconciliation. In other words, God in Christ was reconciling the world to himself, not holding men's faults against them, and he has entrusted to us the news that they are reconciled. (2 Corinthians 5:17-21)

This is the mystery into which we have been called: the mystery of unity, the reconciling of Jew and Gentile, of establishing all in peace (Ephesians 2:13-22). Such reconciliation and unity are basic to those who sing the song of suffering. For only in such reconciliation and unity can one face the suffering rather than be overwhelmed by the chaos present within it.

The Spirit places us at the root of all reconciliation: God, the center of all living things. Much as a wound that heals from the inside out makes for the strongest healing, so those whose reconciliation begins at the deepest point of their existence (God) initiate the most permanent change in their suffering situation. We are enlivened by *the* song we share.

Suffering makes us only too aware of our emptiness. We cry out to be filled, to overcome our loss. We can always choose the old song, never recognizing that the loss we experience in suffering reflects a deeper loss that leaves our entire life one of suffering. We can center our life on those physical, emotional, and social dimensions that we have mentioned so often. Or, if not these, we can look to the God of our pre-suffering life and rest upon that seeming rock. *Or,* we can accept the experience of suffering, flow with it, be moved beyond ourselves in the new song we are conscious of. We can accept this new vision that arises from a basic experience of human life that creates and binds the human community together. We can raise our consciousness to see that *we* are. We exist only in relation to others. We are related to others in active reconciliation. We come into existence as we experience a consciousness and explicit interaction with others. As the psychologist Paul Pruyser says in *A Dynamic Psychology of Religion* (New York: Harper & Row, 1968) our intrapersonal reality deepens as our interpersonal relationships deepen. Or, in the words of the theologian Joseph Powers in *Spirit and Sacrament* (New York: Seabury Press, 1973), we prefer to settle for more being rather than well-being. We are called to fulness of being, the fulness of God himself (Ephesians 3:19). We are called to cosmos and reconciliation within yet beyond this suffering. The new song, the new Spirit, reveals us to ourselves: We are not alone. Suffering is diminished only as this realization takes over our whole life and reconciliation begins. Such realization is called love.

This is the Spirit of love. Love is the first result of this new song (Galatians 5:22-23). The others are joy, peace, patience, kindness, goodness, faithfulness, gentleness, and self-control. St. Paul describes love this way:

> Love is patient; love is kind and envies no one. Love is never boastful, nor conceited, nor rude; never selfish, not quick to take offense. Love keeps no score of wrongs; does not gloat over other men's sins, but delights in the truth. There is nothing love cannot face; there is no limit to its faith, its hope, and its endurance.
>
> Love will never come to an end. . . . In a word, there are three things that last for ever: faith, hope and love; but the greatest of them all is love. (1 Corinthians 13:4-8,13, NEB)

Love is the admittance of "we," for every song needs both singer and hearer. The deepest song is founded on a "we" that is permanent. Every singer finds that he or she is both singer and hearer and much more.

When love forms the song, the hearers acknowledge that they will listen as long as humanly possible; they will hear with their total being; they will share their song. Love is not something of the moment but rather a willingness to be with the other during his or her entire suffering. Love is also not of the emotions alone but of the total person, mind and body. Love, finally, focuses upon the other, not upon the self. Suffering must find love as one of its dimensions. Only in the presence of love will suffering be significantly diminished. As love deepens, suffering diminishes, though it never disappears.

That is why this new consciousness is also the Spirit of promise. Suffering surfaces the hope of reconciliation among the body, emotions, self, and others. The Spirit shows that this hope is not in vain but that the promise of total peace and reconciliation—sometimes called heaven—will always be ours. Our experience of suffering shows that suffering is always to some degree present; thus as one way of suffering diminishes, another comes to take its place. The promise of the Spirit, based on Jesus' resurrection, is that there will be a time of resurrection-life when suffering will be destroyed. We see hints of the fulfillment of the promise whenever suffering is diminished. Such a promise, as Moltman mentions in his *Theology of Hope* (New York: Harper & Row, 1967), announces the coming of a reality that does not yet fully exist; that binds people to the future, giving them a sense of history; that gives history itself a definite trajectory and thus makes time sacred; that bases our evaluation of present realities on the future, not on the past. The Spirit of promise gives such a context to suffering that our present suffering is an announcement of a world to come; the community of suffering is inspired to diminish suffering; our moments of suffering become sacred as loss is filled with reconciliation; our evaluation of our suffering and that of others awaits the total story to be told in the promised world.

Such a Spirit is not a comfortable one. Promise, love, reconciliation, unity in the midst of chaos can hardly be willed. That is why this Spirit is indeed the Paraclete. He is our comforter, intercessor, and advocate. The Spirit, like the song, is ourselves yet something more. It is this "more" that enables us to share our new song with so many.

The Spirit present in suffering is that Spirit we call Holy. It is not a spook or ghost. It is not "spiritual" in the sense of being our better self: when we are doing right, praying, going to church, giving alms. The Holy Spirit is our center, the deepest dimension of our life. It is that dimension out of which we see and experience the world around us and out of which we act. It is the context or background that makes sense of our life. It is, as the theologian Paul Tillich says, the ground of our being. Some church Fathers went so far as to describe the Spirit as the soul of the Christian life, for only when we enjoy the life of God, grace, can we say "Abba" (Father), be a son or daughter of the Father, and enter heaven. The Spirit is the context for life. Finally, as the eighth chapter of Romans says so well, the Holy Spirit is the presence of Jesus among us.

The Song Present in Mystery

The experience of hope indicates that we have not obtained the object of our hope. Yet we could not hope unless this object were among us in some way. It is as if, enlivened by a song, we look forward to a deeper experience shared by more people: We would not know what to hope for unless we had already experienced it in some way. The Spirit is the guarantor of the future. We have grasped a part of the future in our consciousness of the Spirit's presence. This is indeed a holy consciousness. The Spirit is present, but not fully, since what we are conscious of is not complete. The time between the now and the not yet is the time of mystery.

Mystery here is to be understood in two senses: *the unknown* and *the manifestation of life's basic realities*.

The Spirit's presence is *unknown* in the sense that it is not clearly evident to the senses. We must discover it by being conscious of what our senses tell us in a different way. Just as the pictures in our example could have been used to tell many different stories, so the experience of the world conveyed by our senses can be understood differently. Suffering is one experience, among many, that uncovers the hidden so that we can understand the real context of life: the conflict between cosmos and chaos. Yet this context is constantly changing in the light of all that is involved in a suffering situation. The Spirit gives us the capacity for the experience, vision, and hope of God the Father. Yet the totality of the experience, vision, and hope is never complete, and thus the Spirit is never totally known.

The time between the now and the not yet is also a time of mystery because it is *the symbolic manifestation of life's basic realities* in such a way that it reinforces them by creating a new situation. Mystery in this sense is a sacrament. A sacrament is a means by which we feel, touch, and hear that which, in its totality, is beyond sensation. These realities become alive for us in the sharing. What enlivens us to life's totality is beyond what we can immediately document. It points beyond ourselves in space and time. It harkens to a shared past, present, and future. It manifests some of the deepest realities in our life. The Eucharist, for instance, is a manifestation of praise and thanks to the Father for what he has done, is doing, and will do among us. It is much more than the prayer over bread and wine that is seen with the consciousness-raising we call faith. We experience Jesus among us—Jesus who is the source of life.

Suffering is also mysterious. Suffering throws us into life's unknowns: How will we get through it? How will others react? What will be the result upon our bodies? Will it ever be over? How will life be once all this is over? Suffering is filled with unknowns. This is its chaotic nature. Suffering is also mysterious as sacrament or manifestation. It manifests and reinforces our "lostness." Whenever we suffer we do so because of a specific loss. But our suffering is more than one loss; it is the sacrament of "lostness." This "lostness" is consecrated, so to speak, by bringing us into the presence of the spirit of Jesus, the Jesus who was "lost" for others. The sacrament of lostness is a manifestation of chaos in the midst of cosmos, of loss in the midst of gain, a basic reality of every life. In the very act of manifesting loss there is present a new consciousness of need and fulfillment; of brokenness and reconciliation; of gain in the midst of loss. Our new song is present in this mystery of suffering.

Limits and Challenges:
The Spirit's Hiddenness

Every sacrament is limited; that is one reason why sacraments are so well fitted to our human (limited) nature. Sacraments act as a bridge between what is finite and what is infinite. Thus while suffering calls attention to our limits, as every sacrament does, it also brings to consciousness who or what is limiting us, the other side of the bridge. For suffering is the result of limitation: a sudden inability to use the body that functioned so well in the past, an increasing inability to communicate with one's spouse, a lonely life of misunderstood intentions and desires.

Suffering is a situation where the dominant presence in the song we sing enlivens few and has even fewer listeners. The eyes of those who listen are dull. We may feel we cannot do anything about the suffering situation. We know we must adapt and sing our song in a new way, but we feel helpless to begin. Somehow we must hear the songs of others and share theirs. Somehow ours must be heard anew for us to step away from the kind of suffering that may leave us with no song to sing. But we cannot. A power or presence must enliven our song before it can be heard. Of ourselves we can do nothing. We are limited. That which is beyond our limits but part of them must provide the presence.

This limitedness of suffering is difficult to accept. We are constantly challenged to change, to acknowledge ignorance, to reject feelings of omnipotence, to be free, to yield, and to love in the midst of mystery.

To change is the challenge of suffering. Limits suddenly come upon us without any wish on our part. As singers of the song of communal suffering, we may be challenged by the prophets in our midst to acknowledge an unjust structure and accept the suffering necessary to change it. We never know when we can share the song of another in mutual suffering. As our society begins to shout in response to severe economic pressure, many will be crying for change. The challenge of the change that results from suffering is to see whether the Spirit is present in this change or not.

To acknowledge partial ignorance in the face of suffering is essential: It takes courage to say we do not know, rather than to speak lies or half truths. It is a brave step to admit our limitations and therefore our ignorance.

Which brings us to the most significant challenge: to reject the desire of personal omnipotence. To reject such a desire is both admission of limit and rejection of infinite power. We do not have such power, even the kind suggested by the following story.

A group of children were playing with a dead fish: They poked at its eyes, beat its body, covered it with sand, washed it, used it as a ball for their bat. All-powerful, they "proved" their power by exulting in the weakness of one of God's creatures.

Sometimes we are like those children. We may admit with our minds that we are limited, but our whole self hates to admit that we are not all-powerful. But knowing that we cannot create like a god, we destroy like a god. We bind together our limitations in an effort to be omnipotent. As Otto Rank suggests in *Will Therapy and Truth and Reality* (New York: Knopf, 1936), the death fear of the ego is lessened by killing or sacrificing the other; through the destruction of the other we buy ourselves freedom from the penalties of dying, of being killed. Like the children we cry out, "I'm all-powerful! See how I can destroy!"

The challenge is to face the dragon of suffering: to turn and face our suffering straight on, to see we are limited. In this acknowledgment we will be free. Then we will not have to destroy. Instead of egotistically demanding that only our song be sung, we can admit we have little control. In this admission we feel the presence that enlivens all songs. An admission of being limited by four walls and no longer beating against them with our hands enables us to walk freely and use our hands to create. In recognizing our finitude we recognize who we are. The craving for total knowledge or control only destroys our enjoyment, our authentic relations, and our dependencies upon others.

In such an admission we yield, we let down our guard and admit we are dependent upon others. To admit we are not the sole cause of our life opens us up to the life of others. To admit the necessity of hearing the songs of others is to share our song with them.

Such yielding and sharing can result from our loving ourselves and others. Our limitations are our challenge. But suffering manifests both our love and the love of God among us. To be conscious of unlimited love we must be conscious of our limitations. Until we know we are creatures we cannot know the creator. Suffering gives us an opportunity (which we can of course reject): the opportunity to raise our consciousness in the realization of a new consciousness, the holy consciousness of the Spirit.

Conclusion

A new consciousness makes us aware that the Holy Spirit is present in suffering. We do not claim that this awareness is evident to everyone, because we realize the gratuitousness of this consciousness-raising activity. But as we look at the themes that concluded Part One, we realize that these can be seen as ways of describing the presence of God's Spirit.

The experience of suffering makes us aware of our shared humanity when we realize that we all suffer and are responsible for one another's suffering. Such realization and responsibility lead us deeper into the significance of our limitations and powerlessness before the chaos that is also present in suffering.

The reality of our shared suffering can be understood from

another perspective: the Christian one. From this perspective the source of this feeling and understanding of our shared suffering is the Holy Spirit.

The Spirit raises our consciousness, as suffering does. The Spirit reconciles what is divided. Suffering will diminish only as reconciliation takes place. Love is the Spirit's means of reconciliation. Suffering, if resolved at its deepest level, will be totally overcome only through love. As reconciliation takes place, community is formed. The community of suffering is reflected in the Spirit's community of reconciliation. We saw, therefore, that the major themes of the suffering experience are matched by the major themes interpreting the reality of the Holy Spirit.

In this chapter we picked up the various pictures of suffering as found in experience and suggested that the story they tell is the story of the Spirit's presence among us. The next chapter will look at the God in whose presence this Spirit places us.

* * *

Questions for Individual Reflection
1. Do you look forward to the end of suffering?
2. Do you do anything to hurry its end?
3. Name two things you hope for.
4. Are they for you alone, or for others?
5. Are you conscious of the Spirit's presence?

Questions for Group Reflection
1. Do you know anyone who sings the songs presented in Part One? Has their suffering made them different?
2. Do you agree that everyone suffers; that we do not suffer alone; that we are responsible for causing our own and others' suffering; that we are limited?
3. What does it mean to love others? How can our various singers show their love while suffering?
4. Will suffering ever end? Is the real world the world of suffering, or of happiness?
5. What are the signs of the Spirit's presence?

CHAPTER SIX

The Source of Song, The Maker of Keys

*"The language of the cross may be illogical to those who are not on
the way to salvation, but those of us who are on the way see it as God's
power to save. . . . Where are any of our thinkers today? Do you
see now how God has shown up the foolishness of human wisdom? If
it was God's wisdom that human wisdom should not know God, it
was because God wanted to save those who have faith through the
foolishness of the message that we preach. And so, while the Jews demand miracles and the Greeks look for wisdom, here are we
preaching a crucified Christ; to the Jews an obstacle that they cannot
get over, to the pagans madness, but to those who have been called,
whether they are Jews or Greeks, a Christ who is the power and the
wisdom of God. For God's foolishness is wiser than human wisdom,
and God's weakness is stronger than human strength."*

—*1 Corinthians 1:18,20-25*

* * *

Can any consciousness free us from suffering? Can any presence?
If so, which consciousness, which presence? Which consciousness can reach to the root of suffering and change it?
Where is the ability to change the water of suffering into the
wine of joy? To be without a song is to be mute, destroyed by suffering. Who or what can provide us with a song to sing that is truly ours? Who or what is the source of song, the maker of keys?

If suffering is chaos, emptiness, nothingness, we know of one
who is capable of bringing cosmos and meaning from chaos and
meaninglessness. In Christianity we use the word "God" to indicate the one who creates cosmos. The Spirit is God's presence
among us.

The word "God" is a symbol, as every word is, of a
community's experience in relationship to a particular reality. As
a symbol it has many meanings, all of which have some relationship to the reality it expresses. It is not unusual, though, that one
meaning will predominate at one historical moment, another

meaning at another moment. For example, the word "woman" has different significant meanings depending upon one's stage of life. "Woman" may signify to us mother, wife, lover, executive secretary, student, teacher—depending upon whether we are a two-year-old, husband, young adult, male president, teacher in an all-girls' school, or a student in a school staffed entirely by women. The word "rule," too, has one meaning when there are only dictators and another at the time of TV presidencies. To "rule," for the dictator, is to be the omnipotent controller of everything that happens in a nation; to "rule," for the president of the United States, is to encourage people to act. Finally, the word "love" means something quite different in a male-dominated culture admitting polygamy as compared to what it means in a North American culture brought up on romantic movies and the "soaps." Words, while referring to something real, refer to quite different aspects of that reality at various times and places. The word "God" is no different from other words in that respect.

The word "God" as we use it and it is understood today is the result of a long historical development. There is quite a distance between the first beliefs of the early Jews and the highly sophisticated distinctions of contemporary thinkers. When I speak of God in the discussion below I will be dependent upon what is called Process Theology. Process Theology is a theological movement that emphasizes God's love of us rather than his uncreatedness. It also emphasizes, as will be seen, that humanity, God, and world are in a mutual process of development. Process Theology takes our holistic nature seriously. It also takes the scriptural description of God and of Jesus as the expression of God seriously. If you wish to read more I would suggest Norman Pittenger's *Unbounded Love: God and Man in Process* (New York: Seabury Press, 1976) and John B. Cobb, Jr., and David Roy Griffin's *Process Theology: An Introductory Exposition* (Philadelphia: The Westminster Press, 1976).

We have hinted at a consciousness in which we may speak of God—the new consciousness brought on by suffering. We have suggested, too, that an essential dimension of this new consciousness is an awareness of a presence that is the source of meaning and coherence. This new consciousness may make us aware of something about God that we may have never realized: that he shares our suffering, for he is present with us. Let us first look at this God who shares our suffering and then reflect upon the place of God in our experience of suffering.

A Suffering God

Which God is the source of the Spirit's presence? Which God can deliver us from the chaos of suffering? Who cares for us, not for just a moment, like a drug that masks deep pain for a few hours, but forever? Which God treats us as human? Which God takes suffering seriously? Which God shares suffering in order to diminish it? The God of Jesus does. Some describe Jesus as if he were separate from God, acting to tell us about someone other than himself who really is God. And *that* God, not Jesus, is eternal, separate, and aloof from us. Jesus is found, in these theories, pointing upward to a God out there rather than being God himself.

But this is not so. Jesus and the Father are one. He who sees Jesus sees the Father. He who sees this man crying, sweating, angry, and dying, sees God. Jesus, who is God, delivered and delivers us from our suffering by sharing it deeply. Through this loving sharing he begins the reconciliation of all things and peoples.

He suffered in his life as well as in his death. He was rejected by the people he grew up with (Matthew 11:20-24), who became convinced that they did not want him around (Matthew 13:53-58). Those in the capital rejected him. He spent his whole life telling the people about God's purpose for us and bringing it about through his miracles. They rejected him, his teachings, and his miracles. The people walked away from him (John 6), even tried to stone him (John 8:59). The "church" of that time challenged the truth of what he said, and his authority to teach (Matthew 21:23-27). The officials put him to death. Everyone who counted was against him.

He had some friends, one of whom died. He cried over his friend's death (John 11). There were other friends: women, some of them former prostitutes; very young idealists, such as John; ignorant fishermen, such as Peter; crafty tax collectors, such as Matthew, who represented the oppressive foreigners. The down-and-out were his friends: a group of misfits and rejects of society; a crowd of people whom the priests and teachers described as drunks, lawbreakers, and gluttons.

Because of the people he associated with, what he said, and what he did, Jesus was made to suffer. Too many times we forget the *continual* suffering in Jesus' life. In the midst of the rejection by the learned, the powerful, and the holy, he felt that he was going to die (Mark 8:31; Mark 9:31; Matthew 17:22). This "baptism," as he called it, seemed to be in his consciousness. As a man with terminal illness sometimes recognizes that his time is near, so it seemed that Jesus felt his time was near.

It was indeed near. Jesus was newsworthy for only a few years; within a short time he was captured and killed. The story of Jesus' condemnation and execution is one we have heard so often that we easily forget what occurred.

From our perspective as Christians, we believe Jesus was innocent of what he was condemned for by both church and state. We believe that what happened to him was completely unjust. We can easily forget that in Jesus we have an example of human suffering in which a young man in the prime of life is unjustly and savagely murdered by the state to save itself from political pressure.

What happened? All his friends left him after one close friend turned him in to the authorities. When he was captured he was beaten, made fun of, dressed in fool's clothes, and spat on. He was brought before the judges, but even though his fate was determined, they had to twist the law to kill him. One judge, Pilate, offered him a chance to escape, and he did not take it. Pilate also tried to get the people gathered for the judgment to let Jesus go, but they rejected Jesus and chose to set Barabbas free. They really cannot be blamed. Jesus' reputation among the majority was terrible: He was breaking the laws—especially the one that prohibited working on the Sabbath; he was thought to be possessed by the devil; he hung around with troublemakers; everyone who had ever lived with him, including many of his former disciples and townspeople, now wanted nothing to do with him. It was even rumored that his mother was a prostitute. He was just no good! What he said started riots, and what he did questioned the laws of God and of religion. Better to get rid of him.

He died as many other criminals did: naked and nailed to a cross. For some reason he refused the drugged wine (Mark 15:23) offered to him and died in a shorter time than most crucified criminals.

What did Jesus talk about during his public life? The Gospels tell us his "good news." What did he do? The Gospels show us his miracles. The Gospels also show us some of his feelings: anger at Jerusalem for rejecting him, grief over his friend's death, and sadness over the people's rejection of him and his message. He seemed willing to sustain the suffering while hoping, praying, it would go away. The temptation scene in the desert shows him hungry, thirsty, and humiliated, yet not taking the means to lessen his suffering. He faces suffering and somehow seems to absorb it. He does not want to suffer or die. The scene in the Garden makes this point clearly: "Father, if you are willing, take this cup away from me. Nevertheless, let your will be done, not mine" (Luke 22:42). He was afraid. He sweated. He did not want to suffer. But he did. And in suffering he felt totally the abandonment of God: "My God, my God, why have you deserted me?" (Mark 15:34). Pinned to the cross, abandoned by his friends, in deep physical pain, he feels the depth of the chaos of suffering: the loss of purpose, of meaning, of a reason for living—the loss of God.

In the depths of these losses we find God. Absurd? No. Jesus is God. God does not just preach to us, perform miracles, be born of a virgin. No, God walks this earth, suffers, and dies. "God can't suffer," we might say. But Jesus did. "God is powerful; he could have destroyed them all," we might say again. But Jesus *is* God. Somewhere in the story of Jesus we have to accept the fact of his suffering and death. The Greeks thought it illogical that a God could die. Many Jews of that time also thought that one who claimed to be God should perform miracles rather than be put on a cross to die like a common criminal. We may be like them if we reject God suffering like a human. If we do, we forget that Jesus is both divine and human. Jesus is the manifestation of God among us. And he shows himself as a suffering servant.

> He grew up before the Lord like a young plant
>   whose roots are in parched ground;
> he had no beauty, no majesty to draw our eyes,
>   no grace to make us delight in him;
> his form, disfigured, lost all the likeness of a man,
>   his beauty changed beyond human semblance.
> He was despised, he shrank from the sight of men,
>   tormented and humbled by suffering;
>   we despised him, we held him of no account,
>   a thing from which men turn away their eyes.
> Yet on himself he bore our sufferings,
>   our torments he endured,
> while we counted him smitten by God,
>   struck down by disease and misery;
> but he was pierced for our transgressions,

> tortured for our iniquities;
> the chastisement he bore is health for us
> and by his scourging we are healed.
> He was afflicted, he submitted to be struck down
> and did not open his mouth;
> he was led like a sheep to the slaughter,
> like a ewe that is dumb before the shearers.
> Without protection, without justice,
> he was taken away. . . .
>
> (Isaiah 53:2-5,7-9, NEB)

Ours is a suffering God. He shares with humanity one of its deepest realities, the song of suffering. He does so, not because he loves suffering, but because he loves us. Jesus' suffering was avoidable. The story of his passion shows this: He could have allowed himself to be helped; he did not have to go to Jerusalem or take the political stand he did; he could have avoided confrontation; he could have stopped breaking the Sabbath; he could have talked to Pilate. He could have, but he did not. Jesus in Gethsemane opted for the way of the cross because he opted throughout his life to lead us to freedom and faith (the new consciousness). He spoke the words of good news. He spoke reconciliation and brought it about: He formed a people dedicated to loving others as the Father had loved them, spoke words of reconciliation by forgiving sins, spoke words about life's purposes. These words and actions resulted in suffering and death, as words and actions of liberation often do. Jesus did not suggest that we passively accept suffering, but he accepted the suffering necessary to reconcile us to life's deepest meaning. If he had avoided suffering, he would have avoided love and reconciliation. But he did not. To live life fully, Jesus had to suffer. He would have been untrue to himself and to his mission if he had not accepted the suffering that was part of his life. He was born to reconcile. To be true to his birth and his mission, he had to live a life that included suffering and death. And any of us who wish to imitate him must live within the shadow of the same cross.

We see divine love in Jesus' suffering. Love is not sentimentality, easy toleration, cheap and undemanding acceptance of anything and everything. It is quite different from that kind of storybook love. It is self-giving, sacrificial activity, suffering concern, enduring joy, readiness to accept and receive from others. Such suffering, which is a manifestation of love, indicates a God who suffers, yes, but who also loves. At the very center of our universe, then, are life and love, not coercive power. As Process Theology demonstrates, our obedience, service, and worship have to do with a God who is love. He knows suffering. He shared and shares it with us. He knows what it is to be delivered from suffering, as he was delivered in the resurrection (Philippians 2:6-11).

We need gods if we are to live. If we do not have them, we create them. We cannot live a life of meaninglessness, a life without value and direction. In ways both subtle and not so subtle, we either accept meaning or give our life meaning. A nation gives meaning to its life by re-creating its history time and again. A person shows his or her life to be meaningful by telling his or her story from a perspective that depends upon his or her values and convictions. A god is like a nation's history or a person's story in the way it gives unity, meaning, and purpose to any life. A god is the ultimate value around which our life pivots. A god brings cosmos out of the chaos of scattered events and meanings. Jesus suffers and is God; to accept him as one who suffers is to accept suffering as a way of understanding life.

This God is present in the new consciousness that discloses the Holy Spirit. The love that binds us through the Spirit is the love of God. The movement of the Spirit is the movement of God deepening the reconciliation of each of us to the world and to the people around us, making us a community of life and suffering, a symphony of song, which is the purpose of this world. By sharing our suffering, Jesus gives us a new song to sing. By going before us to lead a resurrected life, he gives us his Spirit as the source of life. He shows us what life and suffering are all about.

A Suffering God and the Songs of Suffering

Our songs of suffering are songs of loss and disintegration. The slow advancement of amyotrophic lateral sclerosis (Lou Gehrig's disease) and the gradual abandonment of memory and consciousness in cerebral arteriosclerosis are vivid portraits of disintegrating bodies and minds. Many disintegrating personalities and families are seen when persons lose their jobs because of a changing economy. As they search for a new job over the years, they gradually lose their possessions, their self-image, and perhaps their friends. Where is the suffering God when St. Helens blows up, when millions of Jews are murdered, when tribe after tribe of Africans starves to death? Where is this God when you and I suffer?

I don't think I can give a coherent and completely logical answer to these questions. Many have tried. Dorothee Soelle's *Suffering* (Philadelphia: Fortress Press, 1975), Michael Galligan's *God and Evil* (New York: Paulist Press, 1976), John Hick's *Evil and the God of Love* (New York: Harper & Row, 1978, 2nd ed.), Jürgen Moltman's *The Crucified God* (New York: Harper & Row, 1976), are a few you may want to read for an answer. I have suggested all along that suffering can only be dealt with holistically. Thus I would suggest that instead of responding to the questions directly, we reflect upon these songs in the light of the experiences or ways of being conscious that we have hinted at up to this point.

An Experience of Nature

The seasons indicate that there is a time for everything (Ecclesiastes 3). People die, and others are born. Trees fall, and others grow. Out of the decomposition of natural things springs new life. We see in nature that there are general patterns of life and death or of disintegration-integration, but we also see that we can never be sure of what will happen in a particular case. The oak tree outside my window may fall, but whether another oak tree or daisies will grow out of the rot is uncertain. But something will grow. Change will occur, and something will come out of that change. We may consider the "something" to be good or bad, to be something we like or something we do not like. Part One showed that when we sing a song of suffering we are involved in change and that the more radical the suffering, the more probable it is that the change will be radical. And so it is in nature. The old passes away. The new takes its place, but we never know for sure if it is for better or for worse until it is over. Yes, life on this earth is always changing, never over. But for its direction, if there is one, we must look elsewhere.

A Faith Experience

A Christian's faith experience is joined to Jesus' experience of death and resurrection. In baptism the Christian joins Jesus' death and resurrection (Romans 6:1-11). This reality of Jesus' death and resurrection colors the Christian's life and interpretation of all experience. Out of Jesus' death and disintegration came the integration of a new and different life. Out of the disintegration and chaos of Jesus' suffering on Good Friday came the life of resurrection on Easter Sunday. The suffering God is also the God of life. Nature's pattern of change and new life resulting from disintegration is reflected in Jesus' death and resurrection.

A Religious Experience

Life is filled with ordinary moments and special moments. The ordinary moments are spent in regular work, play, eating, sleeping. The special ones are remembered, cherished, impressed on our way of being. These special moments are described by some authors as moments of religious experience, times that have about them a feeling of what Rudolf Otto calls *the numinous*, an experience in which we feel overwhelmed and attracted to the source of the experience. It is a moment when we feel that what we are experiencing is much larger than we are. It is more powerful, it is capable of destroying us, it is fearful. Yet we like this experience and what causes it. We feel we would like to feel this presence all the time. Such a presence may be found as the disintegration and chaos of suffering become the integration and cosmos of a new way of living: as death gives way to resurrection. The moment when a person is aware of the presence of love and concern in the midst of suffering is a moment when suffering is conquered. It is a special moment of life in the midst of destruction. Our songs of suffering have such moments. The suffering God is present in suffering and in those moments when suffering ceases. Our challenge is not only to experience the suffering but to be aware of when the special moments are present, for they indicate that there will be a time when this moment without suffering will become an eternity of love.

An Experience of Love

How do we recognize those moments of love and concern in the midst of suffering? Certainly an ascetical life helps us recognize them. The psychologist Erik Erikson also suggests that our past experience of trust helps us recognize and receive love. An infant who has been able to trust those close to him or her will more than likely grow up a trustful person. Someone who has been distrusted and never able to trust others will probably be very pessimistic about human relationships. The moments of love and goodness present in suffering will be harder for the latter person than for the former. But our faith also has a part to play in discerning the presence of love in suffering. We believe that Jesus was not totally abandoned on the cross. We believe that love is present even in the midst of suffering because that was the experience of Jesus.

In the depths of suffering we may easily see ourselves as abandoned and forsaken by everyone. With Jesus we cry "My God, my God, why have you forsaken me?" Everything that gives us meaning seems lost. Life seems empty and void. The paths that lead to this experience of annihilation that occurs in such mute suffering are the same as the destruction found in nature and in the dying of Jesus. But in the depths of this nothingness, deep in the hell of chaos, is love, urging us to cry out, to "reach out and touch someone," to see that life does have cosmos: unity, meaning, purpose. It was in such a descent into "hell" that Jesus was filled with new life, the life of resurrection. Working within each of us, always, is the same life. Suffering in us, in others, speaks chaos, hell, but it also speaks life and love. This is a healing love, a love that respects the singer of songs. It is a love that urges us and hopefully evokes from us a realization of life's purpose and meaning. It is the love found in Jesus.

An Experience of Hope

What do we hope for in our suffering? Most of us know what we don't want. We don't want the hungry to starve, we don't want the divorcée to be lonely, we don't want the sufferer of Lou Gehrig's disease to go through the disintegration of his or her body. But what do we hope *for*? What is the new life that we wish for when this particular song of suffering ceases? I ask this because hidden in the answer is the way we question our present suffering.

Do we hope for no suffering? If our conclusion to Part One is correct, attaining this is impossible in the world as we know it. Do we hope we can be as we were before the suffering? This too is impossible. Are we looking forward to a better life than we have as we sing our song? Such a hope seems to make sense.

But what is a "better" life? Somehow this "better" life should be consistent with the experiences and the songs of suffering we have described. It should acknowledge the singer of songs while looking forward to a time when the songs of suffering will never be sung. Such a life can be founded on a God who brings about a better life by suffering with us in the past and the present. The term we use to describe such a life is the Kingdom of God. We hope the Kingdom will come and God's will will be done now and forever.

The Experience of the Kingdom and Easter

The very nature of suffering speaks of relationship and reconciliation. The sacrament of suffering leads to an integration of the suffering community and the coming of the Kingdom. It leads to the harmony of a community rather than to the sameness of uniformity. The manifestation of love present in the suffering situation comes from all those involved in it. Somehow the love of others speaks to the love within us and calls us to a new life. Love speaks to love, as God's purposefulness is worked out through the pattern of death and resurrection. Our new life in suffering is not a private hurt but one dependent upon others. Suffering manifests the community of chaos as well as the community of life. Both are shared.

But the hell referred to earlier is, strangely enough, in the very sharing, in the movement from death. This is the time of marginality, of doubt, of uncertainty as to what the new life will be. Everyone in a suffering situation is aware of it and experiences it in varying degrees. This hell is a time of shadows and mistaken gods, a time of false starts and purposelessness. It is this because, as Ernest Becker said in *Denial of Death*, "To suffer one's death and to be reborn is not easy. And it is not easy precisely because so much of us has to die." The intensity of suffering is the intensity and comprehensiveness of death and rebirth: of acknowledging what is dead and of remaking broken and lost relationships to the world around us.

To be born again is to be subjected to the terrifying truth of the human condition that we are not born as gods but as humans. To be born again is to be born realizing that suffering is still part of our future. But our new birth, if it is in touch with the center of our life, is part of the wave of love flowing on to the shores of the universe.

To realize the Spirit's presence in suffering is to realize that our suffering is not a once-and-for-all event but a manifestation of an essential part of life as we know it. Death and resurrection is not a once-and-for-all happening in our lives or in the life of every human being. It is instead a dynamic pattern of life itself. The themes of Easter are the experiences of nature and faith. Jesus' death and resurrection manifested these themes in such a way that people understood Easter anew. The yearly celebration of Easter tells us that our suffering and our rebirth will never end as long as this earth groans in chaos stretching toward cosmos. The yearly celebration of Easter places us in the presence of that mystery of Christ's suffering in which we still share (Colossians 1:24; Romans 8:17) and in the presence of the resurrection that is gradually coming about.

We can fear Easter because it is a reminder of suffering and new life. We realize that love is not easy. We realize that to become more than we are, we must have the courage to leave behind what we are and have become for a promise of new life. Every suffering event is filled with the fear and challenge of Easter dawn (Matthew 28:1-6): What is behind the rock guarding the tomb? How will the rock be moved? Is there death, or life, behind it? Suffering challenges us to acknowledge our own Easter fear.

We can avoid this fear by building devices that we hope will protect us from radical newness: dreams of how great a person we are; laughter at how fragile the world is; intellectual constructs explaining the coherence and truthfulness of the well-being that was ours before the suffering. Business and work can help us avoid decision-making. By means of such devices we cover the real chaos within. The new consciousness present through suffering manifests the loss of our self as we know it and the deepening of that loss through fear. We face the Easter rock trembling about what is behind it.

Suffering is not neutral. We can choose not to remove the rock; we can choose to remain as we are: suffering. Or we can choose to remove the rock. But there is suffering even then, because resurrection demands rebirth. New life is not easy. Suffering is going to happen. The question is, will it be the cross of Christ, or the cross of meaninglessness? A future will develop out of present suffering. But will it be the future of chaos, or of cosmos? A suffering that gives birth to chaos is one based on fear, speechlessness, aggression, blind hate. It springs from despair rooted in the feeling that our past, present, and future belong to someone else. Suffering that chooses to remove the rock—to face new being rather than old well-being—chooses to live conscious of our oneness with the whole of life. It chooses to go through the agony of being reborn—a pattern set for us by that first Easter.

The choice is founded in a sensitivity to our individual and communal past. We have had experiences that agree with the course of nature and the songs of suffering. These experiences help us realize that suffering always calls us to a new consciousness and new beginnings.

As believers we know of God's saving acts in the past, and because of this we choose not to run away from suffering but to trust in God's love. We do not seek to escape into the chaos of suffering but to make a new beginning. We do not avoid crisis; we have faith in the future.

The new consciousness does not eliminate risk nor guarantee that we will be able to foresee how the whole pattern of events will develop. All it can do for us is give us strength to make a new beginning, to set out toward an unknown future. We set out because we remember that God is present in judgment and mercy, catastrophe and happiness, death and resurrection. We have seen it time and time again. We have seen it especially in those significant persons who still touch us with their suffering.

Conclusion

As we sing our song of suffering we hurt. We don't want to suffer. We want deliverance. Which of us, upon singing a song of suffering, wants to continue with the song? But how can we be delivered? How can the song of suffering become the song of joy? In Part One we suggested many ways to reduce suffering. But in this chapter we saw that added to these must be a willingness to inquire about the means we use to reduce suffering. Jesus suffered rather than abandon his mission. There were other values and people that were more important than diminishing his own suffering or avoiding death.

We may have been astonished at the suggestion of process theologians that God suffers. There are many very good theological reasons for hesitating to accept such a claim. But it may also be that we hesitate before God's suffering because we live in a culture in which escape from suffering is of ultimate importance. To see suffering associated with God, the ultimate, may initiate a conflict between our cultural and our religious values.

I suggest that there are two lessons to be learned from the claim that God suffers with us: (1) that our suffering doesn't separate us from life even if we feel it does; (2) that if we are to be truly delivered from our suffering we must care for the physical, emotional, communal, and religious aspects of the sufferer.

Since the word "God" is another way of referring to that which is the ultimate unity, meaning, and purpose of life, we have found that God is involved with our suffering. We have found that suffering is somehow involved with God's purposes. Even when we feel the pain of separation in our song of suffering, we know in faith that a healing presence is there sharing the dark night of suffering in order to bring the light of love.

This light of love must shine upon the body, the mind, the feelings, the purposes of life. When we hear the song of suffering, we must hear all of it. When we help to diminish it, we must attend to all its parts.

* * *

Questions for Individual Reflection
1. Where is chaos within you? What are you afraid of?
2. Who gives your life some sense? What are your favorite ways for him or her to help your life have meaning?
3. What was your deepest episode of suffering before last year? Do you remember how you were before it began? What was the worst thing about it? Was there any good in it?
4. Are you guilty of causing suffering? To whom?
5. Can you reasonably lessen that suffering? Will you?

Questions for Group Reflection
1. What are the best examples of death-resurrection in your experience?
2. Do you have any examples of something new coming out of suffering? Something good? Something bad?
3. Do you think God can be angry toward you? Do you think God shares your suffering?
4. Which experiences are most significant to you in facing God's place in suffering: the natural, faith, religion, love, or hope?
5. What can the members of your group do to lessen the suffering present in one of the songs?

CHAPTER SEVEN

The Christian Song

"I baptize you in the name of the Father, and of the Son, and of the Holy Spirit."

— *The Rite of Baptism*

"Be sealed with the gift of the Holy Spirit."

— *The Rite of Confirmation*

* * *

All humans suffer. What is different about the Christian sufferer? The principal difference is that the Christian has put death behind. As the sixth chapter of Romans says so forcefully, in our baptism we have died with Christ, we have risen with Christ.

We suffer: Our head hurts, time passes slowly in our loneliness, people are rude to us, our money runs out. Whether we are Christian or non-Christian, these events are the same. Yet sacraments are real, and something happens as a consequence of our involvement in them. Our pain is not destroyed, but it is not the same as the pain of another. Loneliness still haunts us, but there is a certain presence even there. Money with its consequent comfort does not magically appear. Yet the pain, the lack of money, and loneliness gradually lose their sting as we become conscious of the fact that death has lost its sting by Jesus' resurrection and by our share in it through our baptism.

The Christian Response to Suffering

This initiation into Christ's death and resurrection is also an insertion into that life of the Spirit who is present in suffering. This insertion shapes the response of the Christian to his or her suffering. The response is prophetic, accepting, creative, sharing, hopeful, priestly, and respectful.

Prophetic

The Christian sufferer finds that suffering is prophetic to himself or herself and to others. A prophet is one who speaks a truth before the world. The truth the prophet speaks is present in each song of suffering. One song may declare our lack of the necessary medical skills to cope with physical deterioration; another song may challenge us to share our wealth and power with the destitute; still another song may make us feel guilty because we do not want to attend to the singer of the song. All the songs proclaim a common truth: that God—the love that holds us together in the midst of suffering's chaos—is present even in suffering. For whoever feeds the hungry, gives drink to the thirsty, or clothes the naked does so to Jesus, who is identified with the sufferer (see Matthew 25:31-46). This Jesus must be present to the sufferers with whom he is identified as well as to those helping them.

Accepting

When we talk about accepting suffering, we must be careful about what we mean. Let us first see what acceptance is not and then what it is.

To accept suffering does not mean to tolerate it, put up with it, bear it without complaining. Such an acceptance can actually be a destructive, mute suffering. Accepting suffering in this way is to purposefully "accept" being a thing. A thing is not human.

To accept suffering does not mean pulling up the anchor of hope and allowing suffering to deaden our will to live, to love and serve others. Suffering can do these things to us. Yet to accept mute suffering is to accept chaos. The Christian believer is more than a mute sufferer, as initiation into Jesus' paschal mystery makes clear.

When we accept our suffering, we recognize it as a reality in our life and deal with it as such. To do otherwise is to reject the world as it exists, to enter into an imaginary world of our own making, to play the creator rather than the creature.

Many feel that such acceptance is wrong. One friend of mine said that "to accept suffering is to be either a sadist or a masochist. If we accept suffering, we must enjoy it. Suffering is wrong. It must be destroyed! Acceptance only allows suffering to exist." Another screamed over the phone to someone whose husband was dying of cancer: "Don't believe it. God is bigger than disease. Tell God you won't accept it." And some medical personnel are fearful of any talk of acceptance because they think it is a destruction of the will to live.

Acceptance as we have described it, though, is an acceptance of life, not a rejection of it. It is a yes to life as it is rather than to life as it might be. To refuse to acknowledge and accept suffering is to turn in on ourselves, to reject a future, to say we want death rather than the life present in suffering.

Suffering that does not destroy us can teach us to love life all the more, to have a greater readiness for change, to look to the future. But it does this only when we accept it. Sooner or later we must say "That's it" and set about living with our suffering rather than ignoring it.

The first step to accepting suffering is talking about it. This "talking" may be a cry of pain, a shout of revolt, a hand grasping for friendship. But somehow suffering must find a voice. In doing so it moves from the destructiveness of mute suffering to the creativity of human suffering and the songs that life brings.

Creative
Creative suffering may seem at first a dodge to avoid facing up to the cruelty of suffering. This is not so. Look at the songs of suffering. Each of these songs provides us with an opportunity to do it our way: to live after a person has died, to break the walls of loneliness, to break the boredom of life. Suffering provides us with an opportunity to share with God the power to bring life out of chaos. We become co-creators. The man who responded to the nurse in the song of emotional suffering did so with the flick of a tongue: creating, articulating, prophesying, and sharing.

Sharing
To share one's suffering is difficult. Suffering, if it is not manipulation, reveals our private self to the public. Our body, our weakness, our faults all lie naked before the public eye. If we are poor, we are subject to governmental control of our life, to probing anthropologists and sociological questionnaires; if we are sick, we are naked to nurses, students, nurses' aides, and doctors. Suffering makes us vulnerable. To actively share our vulnerability with others is difficult. Yet others cannot share our suffering unless we are willing to share with them. Sharing is a

two-way street. Even God cannot share our suffering unless we let him. Christian suffering includes Christian sharing.

Hopeful

Christian sharing occurs with a hope that something good will come of it. Hope by its very nature looks to the future. We act for change only with the hope that there will be change. We believe that change is part of the basic purpose of the universe. If God is involved in change, surely our suffering too will pass. Passing, of course, is not enough. We do not hope merely for suffering to pass, but for good to come out of it. A diminishment of suffering is not enough; it must involve a change to a more just and loving situation. The Christian hopes this will happen.

Hope is essential because suffering makes us feel helpless. In the initial stages we can think of little else than being relieved of our suffering. Hope is present in our very act of seeking relief. Hope is not a mental exercise. It is not an emotion. Rather, it is a way of acting in which, standing firm in God's love, we seek the not-yet. And in this act, suffering is diminished.

Priestly

This hope supplies the strength for the Christian to be a priest, a mediator, by mediating his or her new consciousness of suffering's reality to others. For baptism makes the Christian not only prophet but priest. In suffering, the priestly character of baptism finds the Christian clarifying the place of God in suffering. To unbelievers, the sufferer acknowledges the chaos of suffering in order to proclaim the hope of love's victory. To fellow believers, the sufferer mediates what is recognized as God's love, not just love in general. The memory of God's love in the past must be re-membered, put together again, in this particular instance of suffering. The Christian does this by word and deed.

Respectful

Finally, our own response and the response we desire from others is a free one. The Christian, except in some unjust situations, should not force his or her vision upon others. Respect for the singer is essential to sharing his or her song of suffering. Even in unjust situations, the way of nonviolence should predominate. Not every new consciousness born of suffering is a holy consciousness. Even the consciousness of healing love can be part of the old consciousness without the breath of the Spirit. Essential to the Spirit's blowing where it will are respect and freedom. One should rejoice in the vision, offer it to others, but realize that the consciousness of God's love is a gift freely given. Understanding suffering is also a gift. We should respect those who seem to lack that understanding.

The Christian as Saint and Sinner

The Christian sufferer is called to be a saint. This call flows from our having been baptized into Jesus' death and resurrection. But this call, as well as our baptism, is not something that happened in the past with little effect upon the present. No. We are always entering more deeply into our baptism. We are always faced with responding to God's call. We are saints, and yet we are called to be saints. Thus we are always capable of living out those characteristics that manifest the Christian response to suffering. As described earlier, they are idealized descriptions of what we should be and do. The truth is that at times we act in these ways and at other times we do not. The truth also is that God is always present, urging us to become more of what we already are: saints.

The call to sanctity in the songs of suffering helps us realize our sinfulness as well as our limitations. To know the difference between limitations and sin is important for understanding the Christian response to suffering. Having a clear idea of what guilt is can help us know the difference.

Guilt is sometimes thought of as a feeling that we have done something wrong, something sinful. This feeling is many times present in suffering situations. When does it really indicate sinfulness, when not?

In *The Moral Choice* (New York: Doubleday, 1978), Daniel Maguire illustrates the distinction between guilt that points to sinfulness and guilt that does not. He points out that if the lights on the dashboard of a car light up erratically, without any cause, they can be harmful to the driver and other occupants of the car. But if they light up when they are supposed to, they can be a help in the driving and in the protection of that same car. This image helps us understand guilt.

Guilt feelings unconnected to any reality may be unhealthy and can be harmful; they certainly should be looked into. Healthy guilt—true guilt—is another matter, for it indicates areas of responsibility and possible sin. As Maguire defines it, true guilt is "conscious and free behavior (active or passive) which does real unnecessary harm to persons and/or their environment."

We are guilty, in other words, of those wrongful acts we consciously and freely performed or of those obligatory acts we refused to perform. If we cannot control the diet of our spouse, even when he or she knows overeating will result in another heart attack, we are not guilty. If we did not know our marriage partner had certain unfulfilled needs, which ultimately led to divorce, we are not guilty. If 6.5 million Jews died in Hitler's concentration camps before we were born, we are not guilty of their deaths.

We are not guilty when we shoot and kill a person who is unjustly attacking us with a knife. The phrase "real, unnecessary harm" in Maguire's definition points to the fact that even though harm does occur because of our actions, there is no actual guilt unless we inflict the harm unnecessarily. Jesus did harm people: He harmed the sellers in the Temple when he overthrew their tables; he harmed Judas when he refused to turn from his mission; he harmed the pig-herders when he cast out devils and the pigs went into the sea. The core of guilt, then, is (1) real, unnecessary harm coupled with (2) free, conscious behavior. The guilty feeling is an indicator of possible sin, but we must stop and see if this feeling is based on reality.

Guilt is part of many of the songs of suffering. Once suffering begins, we feel guilt for occurrences in the past and present, and even for what may happen in the future. Guilt makes us aware of our freedom and responsibility in the suffering situations. Either we have acted responsibly or we have not.

The feeling of guilt that points to sin helps us answer our call to sanctity. To acknowledge our sinfulness in a suffering situation, to be sorry for what we have done, to ask forgiveness from those we have harmed, and to change our life are all part of hearing God's call and responding to it. The guilt we may feel as we sing a song of suffering should be attended to; it may be a warning that we are not conscious of the Spirit who is present in our suffering. For when the Spirit is present, guilt is overcome by the signs of the Spirit's presence: love, joy, peace, patience, kindness, goodness, fidelity, gentleness, and self-control (see

Galatians 5:22-23, NEB).

Prayer and the Christian

As we have pointed out, Christians should reach out to heal, should struggle to reconcile those forces that pull society apart. They should also pray. Where there is human suffering, there must be human prayer. Prayer today is often either abandoned as escapist or encouraged as the total solution. Some see prayer as a way of running from suffering and the sufferer. When we close our eyes in prayer, they say, we close them to the suffering of others and to our role in alleviating it. So prayer should be avoided, they say. Others, also taking an extreme position, affirm that prayer is all we need to prevent suffering. If we pray with strong faith, they say, we can do anything. Prayer can, after all, move mountains. Contrary to both these perspectives, the new consciousness makes us aware that suffering must find expression in prayer and that authentic prayer always includes suffering.

The difficulty with the position of those who reject all prayer is that they are apathetic. They see no value in putting suffering and life into words. But in fact the sufferer must express and identify his or her own suffering. It is not enough to have someone speak for us. If we cannot speak about our suffering, it will destroy us. It is not important where we find the language or what form it takes, but our lives depend on being able to express ourselves verbally and/or non-verbally. For without the capacity to communicate with others, there can be no change. To become speechless in this sense is to be unrelated; our suffering is mute and isolated. It is death. Suffering must include prayer as an articulation of suffering if suffering is to remain human.

Prayer is one of the traditional ways of putting our situation into words. To reject prayer as illusion is actually to accept the apathy of our age that finds people shrugging their shoulders and exclaiming "What's the use?" This attitude is not the fault of prayer but of our culture which, because of isolation and fear of others, has forgotten the art of sincere communication. The shrug has replaced folded hands.

But even though some reject prayer, a person's dialogue with himself or herself still happens. What is decisive, however, is who the person's dialogue partner is: God, or self. And if it is God, which God? Which pivotal partner does he or she in reality respond to?

The other extreme position affirms that merely by praying to God we can destroy suffering. This is a prayer demanding that God give what he promised to those of faith. Prayer, from this perspective, is merely a chat with God. God becomes a friendly, though powerful, neighbor to whom we can tell all our troubles. He is so interested in our troubles that he will help us—if we believe. But we must believe totally and completely that he will help us. In this view, God helps us by healing us, that is, by performing a miracle that returns us to our former healthy state. Prayer is *the* method we use to cause the miracle to happen. Much as an electric toaster must be plugged in to the socket to make toast, so we must plug in to God to have a healing. Obviously, these people think, suffering is something to be avoided. The purpose of prayer is to keep us the same physically throughout life: to make us healthy, wealthy, and wise. If we never suffer, we must have prayed well.

The difficulty with this approach to prayer is that it neglects the prayer of Jesus at Gethsemane: "Let thy will be done." It turns prayer into magic and God into the giant magician waiting to do his act upon the stage of the world. This is not, as we have suggested, the Christian God. And this understanding of prayer implies that we control God and suffering by our prayer. But our experience of suffering in both singers and songs demonstrates otherwise.

The suggestions that prayer is all we need to deal with suffering and that prayer is senseless in the face of suffering are concepts of prayer and suffering that react with horror to a God who suffers.

Prayer and Suffering
Prayer and suffering are joined in two ways: Suffering can be a prayer, and prayer is necessary when one is suffering.

The characteristics of prayer and suffering are similar because both prayer and suffering are symbolic. Suffering and prayer can be the expression of the person if the person accepts them as such. We can reject suffering by refusing to accept it. We can reject prayer by rejecting God as an illusion. But if we accept suffering as we have described it, we also accept the new consciousness it brings. This consciousness, for the Christian, includes the God-dimension. How we suffer is our reaction to this God-dimension, and this is prayer. It may be bad prayer if we curse, and good prayer if we bless, but it is prayer nevertheless.

Cassian, an early church Father, once said that there is no perfect prayer if the person perceives he or she is praying. Suffering is where Cassian's dictum is most evident, for in suffering we respond from the depths of the self that is formed out of a lifetime. Pain makes analysis difficult or impossible; the sufferer must make his or her way out of the chaos of suffering through trust in the Jesus who shared our suffering and consequently began life anew. This is the prayer of praise: sensing, no matter how minimally, the flow of purpose and love we identify as God and responding to this love by reaching out for the new life we know is present in every suffering situation. Suffering has become prayer.

But prayer is also essential when we are suffering. As has already been suggested, suffering must be articulated to be diminished. Prayer is the beginning of such articulation as the person becomes conscious of his or her feelings and seeks to respond to them. Only inasmuch as there is prayer present is there genuine healing taking place. Prayer puts us in touch with the core of our life. Suffering puts us in touch with what we have lost and what must be healed and reconciled. Prayer begins the healing process from within and builds to include all those relationships that make us human. To know God is to know the way of reconciliation.

The God who suffers with us does not promise a miraculous cure, although it may happen because of particular psychosomatic circumstances. Suffering is diminished not only when a particular pain disappears but also when life is lived in a healthier manner. Suffering disappears as reconciliation occurs. But reconciliation cannot occur unless we freely and lovingly heal those relationships to God, self, others, and things that are weakened as we sing the song of suffering.

The God who suffers responds to our prayer. He responds by offering new life, new consciousness, new beginnings. New life takes shape the way a new song does: out of the forms of the past and of the present. Whether they are musical notations or memories, all forms must be remembered if they are to live again. New consciousness rises from the ashes of the burnt idols of gods who died during our suffering. The new consciousness fills us with the new Spirit.

Prayer and Faith

Faith is a word and an idea that is much abused in talk about suffering and prayer. Sometimes when people encourage us "to have faith," they may think of faith as some type of inner strength or conviction. "Your faith helped you through those difficult days," says the priest to the widow who has cared for a cancer-ridden husband for seven years. "I'm glad we have our faith," proclaim the children of a divorce. "You must have faith or you'll give up," says the doctor. "I wonder what those without faith do in such horrible situations," comments a mother.

Sometimes we talk about faith as if it were a mental muscle: something we must exercise frequently or it will atrophy. We speak of losing it, like losing a wallet or a handbag. What we have faith "in" can vary from faith in ourselves to faith in our doctors or counselors to faith in God. This kind of "faith" is best described as an ability to overlook what is scientifically evident to our senses and mind in order to live at a higher level.

Such "faith" can be evil or good. After all, the business person who has faith in himself or herself may be acting immorally; the faith in an apathetic or masochistic God leads us down a path of confusion and isolation. This kind of faith may actually be a refusal to sing the song of suffering.

What is faith? Faith is the vision of new beginnings that we share with the community of those who believe in the Father as a result of a new consciousness. Implicit in the new consciousness are new beginnings. But these beginnings can be made only if we have the support of others. The Church is where such support is found—or should be found.

The plea for faith in the midst of suffering can be a plea of selfishness: that *I* be healed no matter what the cost. The plea of others for us to have faith in the midst of our suffering can be the demand that we follow *their* God. "You must have faith!" often means "You *must* believe the way *I* do." Faith, like suffering, must be shared to be authentic. Isolated faith—that is, apart from community—is insanity. There is little difference between the individualized imaginings of the insane and that of the "prophets" who prey upon sufferers by demanding faith that calls for blind, unquestioning following of another, whether it be the doctor, the president, or the researcher. These "prophets" tell us not to look at experience, not to share our vision with others, but simply to "believe" in whatever they declare will deliver us. Sad experience has taught us how hollow such promises of deliverance are.

Such "prophets" also seek a security that is not to be found in this life. Faith draws us into an essentially symbolic relationship with life. Faith is not in the realm of scientific analysis. Faith shares life's, not science's, truth. Faith is communal, dynamic, personal, and filled with meaning, as all symbols are. And it is mysterious. A faith or religion that seeks absolute security seeks a life without beginnings, a life where everything is planned, known, secure. But the suffering God offers no such promise. Jesus' acceptance of death and suffering shows us that total security, peace, and prosperity on this present earth are actually descriptions of a kind of hell. For they can come to us only by destroying love, freedom, and concern for others. An absolutely secure future is one without suffering. Such security can be gained only by abandoning the sufferers, an act abhorrent to God.

Faith may be lost in the midst of suffering. We abandon the sufferer, and he or she can lose faith. Chaos becomes so overwhelming that the sufferer is mute, no longer acting in a human way. The sufferer loses the vision, fears new beginnings, and rejects the reconciliation necessary to live anew. Depression is so much a part of suffering that it seems trite to mention it. Yet there is no God-consciousness, no hope, nothing except darkness when we are in deep depression. The God we pray to does not seem to respond or to initiate any new consciousness. Praying is like singing down an empty hall: We hear only our own song. Suffering destroys visions. Suffering destroys communities. Suffering destroys lives. To hear any of the songs, to see any of the singers, is to witness the hell of suffering. To suffer in this way is to live in a night so dark that we see nothing, hope nothing, sense nothing but pain, loss, emptiness. We are abandoned. "My God, my God, why have you deserted me?" (Mark 15:34)

We scream. And in the scream is the beginning of prayer. In the dark night, to risk screaming, to risk moving in some way, is to begin. Deep within us is the urge to begin, to change, to go beyond this moment of suffering. This movement of new beginnings of life is a movement out of chaos toward cosmos. It is the movement of love that seeks union with others. God acts within us. We have faith.

Faith recognizes our shared vision with God and with other Christians. Prayer recognizes what and who is behind what is happening. Suffering surrounds us. Scientific analysis, though necessary, stands ill at ease with its hands on the laboratory table while the sufferer looks for hands extended in friendship and justice. There is no obvious answer to relieve all the suffering shown to us by our singers. But faith shows visions of new beginnings from the past and looks forward to yet newer ones. Prayer is our response to this vision. Together the pray-ers and believers can begin to lessen humanity's suffering. Standing, as Newton said, upon the shoulders of those who have gone before us, we reach for the stars.

Conclusion

The cross is always present. This challenge of reconciliation is always visible. Around it are gathered the forces of chaos and cosmos, death and resurrection. If we accept the challenge, we place ourselves between these two forces. To give a center to what is split or divided, we must stretch in two directions at once. We must struggle with both death and life to bring healing to the sick and wholeness to society.

It could be an exhilarating struggle, an overwhelming experience of oneness, if the split did not reach into the very roots of our being, into the very nature of our Christianity. The cross marks the spot of division as well as of healing. Thus we suffer as individuals and as community to be reconciled as well as to reconcile, to heal ourselves as well as to heal.

In healing and being healed we are prophetic, accepting, sharing, creative, hopeful, priestly, and respectful. We struggle to make our baptism real. But we do not struggle alone. The new consciousness is ours only because of a new Spirit. The Spirit urges us to new beginnings and new consciousness. We pray.

We pray: We sense the flow of purpose and love that we identify as God; we reach out for the new life present in every suffering situation. We pray because we have faith. For faith is the vision of new beginnings that we share with the living and the dead—a vision that stretches from the first moment of human suffering till this moment. In the midst of the vision, as in the midst of the suffering, shines the source of life, the Father, who shares our suffering in his Son and lives with us still in the Spirit. This is the Christian song.

* * *

Questions for Individual Reflection
1. Are you prophetic, accepting, sharing, creative, hopeful, priestly, and respectful?
2. Name one hindrance to being the things listed in the first question.
3. Do you pray? Pray right now.
4. Name two areas in your life that demand a new start.
5. What can you actually do about these two areas this week?

Questions for Group Reflection
1. Do the characteristics of a Christian sufferer make him or her any different from the non-Christian?
2. What is your favorite story illustrating faith?
3. If there is one word to describe how a Christian should suffer, what is it?
4. How should a Christian deal with pain?
5. How should a Christian deal with counselors/psychiatrists?

Conclusion to Part Two

A giant hospital crowns the hill; over it is a cross. . . . A large educational complex of thousands of students and hundreds of millions of dollars stretches like an octopus over the landscape; over it stands the cross. . . . Starving people stretch out their hands for food and comfort; from the neck of the person sharing their food dangles the cross. The cross is found in many places. But it is easy to forget why it is there.

The cross is the symbol of Jesus' act of reconciliation. The songs of suffering plead for reconciliation in whatever form is necessary to heal the wounds of individuals and societies. The cross is still the symbol of reconciliatory action. Jesus in his Holy Spirit has been with us since his resurrection. The cross marks one place this Spirit is active, one place where the old consciousness is seen as a temptation.

One tribe of aborigines in Australia carry around the tent pole of their principal building. They believe that the universe revolves around it. Wherever the pole is planted, there is the center of the world. The pole is the sacred place, the place where the spirits gather, the place of holiness and sacred presences.

The cross is a marker much like the tent pole. Around it are gathered those who are to see in a new way and act out of the newness of what they see. At times those who are conscious of this new vision may lose it. Newness quickly becomes old. It is easy to forget that the cross was placed over a building, hung around a neck, signed on a forehead, or placed at the forefront of a movement to indicate the reconciliation taking place around it.

It is easy to forget where these crosses are in our daily life. "They're not just for churches anymore." Part Two traced the sign of the cross over physical illness, emotional loss, and social disintegration. These three songs of suffering become something more than meets the eye when the chaos of suffering is crossed out by those who share the cross of reconciliation. The Church is the community of those who serve by sharing suffering. It is a community of and for sufferers that offers reconciliation to all.

The Church, at times, has been a countersign to the cross: The sacraments celebrated isolation rather than community, economic power more than poverty, class distinction instead of brotherhood and sisterhood, health rather than sickness. History is filled with religious wars, pompous popes, superstitious laity, and selfish clergy. The days of countersign are not past, though our hope is that they are lessened where the cross marks the spot of suffering and reconciliation.

To plant the cross of reconciliation is what is important when we sing the song of suffering. In Chapter Four we examined many ways of understanding suffering, but we came to realize that only in sharing suffering do we understand it. Only in singing the song of suffering with others do we diminish suffering. How do we know that? We know it because the source of all song, the cause of all life, showed us the way. As Christians we believe that Jesus is both human and divine. As Christians we believe that we humans were alienated from God, from one another, from nature, and even from our own innermost purposes. Jesus showed that the healing of what is broken or alienated occurs in suffering—where the cross is anchored. He marked our path to reconciliation with his cross; we follow him by marking it with our cross so others may follow us.

We follow him when we study to conquer illness, when we help those in grief, when we struggle to create just social structures, when we allow others to share our suffering. We follow him because we are fortunate to be aware of how the suffering of our Good Fridays will find the joy of Easter Sunday and of how the songs of suffering will become the alleluias of eternal life.

APPENDIX

A Song to Sing

As a final reflection upon our life of suffering, I would like to offer you a "song" I have sung a few times in my life. I have shared my song with you as you have read this book. You have shared your song with those in your group or someone you trust. Let us share this song together. It is written for a group; but a solitary, slow, quiet reading done in a reflective manner can still have its solemn moment of sharing.

Leader: *Berakah Yahweh!*

> We praise and thank you for life, Father:
>> for life that cries from the womb to dance, sing,
>> and struggle;
>> for life that chases birds on still summer days and
>> rolls like a snowball in fresh-fallen snow;
>> for life that lies exhausted at day's end from trying
>> too hard;
>> for life that throbs in every heart and mind in
>> this room;
>> for life that creates ever new feelings of love and
>> concern;
>> for life that is shared among us.

First
Speaker: For the life that is, and the life we live.

All: That's all we're asking: Give life a chance.

Leader: Adam lived your paradise life:
>> walked in your presence,
>> ran with arms open wide to embrace your
>> goodness,
> Until one day he closed those arms,
> Took the forbidden fruit,
> And learned of good and evil.
> Life stopped.

And you said:
>   Never again shall you live here.
>   By the sweat of your brow shall you eat.
>   With pain and agony shall you bring forth
>   children.

Second
Speaker: Life began. And we live.

All: That's all we're asking: Give life a chance.

Leader: Noah tended his crops. Life was good.
Noah looked around. Life was evil.
He built an ark: life's refuge.
The world was washed clean of evil.
Life stopped.

And you said:
>   Leave selfishness and terror buried beneath
>   the water.
>   Start new worlds.
>   Open the ark and let life begin.

And two by two the animals marched:
Life in rainbow colors flashed its hues.

Third
Speaker: Life began. And we live.

All: That's all we're asking: Give life a chance.

Leader: A chance is what Abraham wanted.
What he took:
>   The wheel of faith spun and he walked.
Family. Homeland.
Easy ways of thinking and doing.
Secure life.
He left it all. His gods were dead. His world gone.
Life stopped.

But you said:
>   Your seed shall be like the sand of the desert,
>   the stars of the sky;
>   Your life shall be forever.

Fourth Speaker:	And he believed. And we live.
All:	That's all we're asking: Give life a chance.
Leader:	Give us a chance, said Moses. Let your people go. Give them freedom. But Egypt was warm, comfortable, enjoyable. The desert, harsh and bitter. Without life. How could life survive there?

	And you were there, Father,
	    Guiding them in cloud and fire.
	In desperation they sang your praise and petitioned
	    your help to reach the land of milk and honey.

Fifth Speaker:	And they did. They lived. And we live.
All:	That's all we're asking: Give life a chance.
Leader:	Thank you, Father, for life. For the life of all of us. For the life of your people.

	But especially we praise and thank you for the life
	    of Jesus:
	    The child of Mary.
	    The woodworker from Galilee.
	    Joseph's son.
	He lived like all of us, yet was a source of life to
	    those around him.
	He reached out and healed the lame, the blind, the
	    sinners.
	He spoke forgiveness in God's name.
	He taught meaning for daily living.
	He offered us eternal water for eternal thirst.
	Then came a night he offered us bread, not stone.
	The night before he was pounded upon a cross.
	It was on this night that he took bread, blessed it,
	    broke it, and gave it to his disciples, saying:
	    Take, eat; this is my body which will be
	      given up for you.

Then he took the wine and blessed it, saying:
>Take, drink; this is my blood which will be shed for all of you.

Do this in memory of me.

In memory of what he did and does, we live.

We remember.

We gather here today remembering those who have died, who have suffered, who are suffering.

All
(Speak):
We remember and believe that Christ has died, Christ is risen, Christ will come again.

We remember and believe that those who eat your body and drink your blood will live forever.

We remember and believe that you are the God of the living and the dead.

We remember and believe that your life is with us yet.

We remember and believe that broken bodies and broken lives will be made whole.

Here. In re-membering is that life. Your life: reaching out to heal the sick, to speak forgiveness, to present your loving kindness.

Send your Spirit, Lord. Grant us the peace of Adam, of Noah, of Abraham, of Moses. Grant us the peace of Jesus.

That's all we're asking: Give peaceful life a chance.

Through him, with him, and in him in the unity of the Holy Spirit, God, forever and ever.

All
(Sing):
Amen, Alleluia. Amen, Alleluia. Amen, Alleluia.
Alleluia, Amen.

* * *

Leader
(Reflec-
tively):
A song, Lord, a song.
We are never without one as long as we can say Amen.
Shout Alleluia.

All:
Amen, Alleluia.

Leader:
Let us sing of love that reconciles.

All: Amen, Alleluia.

Leader: Let us sing of binding wounds of hate, of pain, of isolation.

All: Amen, Alleluia.

Leader: Let us sing of Jesus who shares our suffering.

All: Amen, Alleluia.

Leader: Let us sing of the Holy Spirit, our Paraclete.

All: Amen, Alleluia.

Leader: Let us sing of *(the names of people in the group).*

All: Amen, Alleluia.

Leader: Let us sing of those who are in pain.

All: Amen, Alleluia.

Leader: Let us sing of those feeling loss.

All: Amen, Alleluia.

Leader: Let us sing of those we cannot help.

All: Amen, Alleluia.

Leader: Let us sing. Amen, Alleluia.

All
(Sing): Amen, Alleluia. Amen, Alleluia. Amen, Alleluia.
Alleluia, Amen.

Leader: We do have a song to sing. Sing it with others!

(All exchange the greeting of peace.)